Bright Ideas
Music

Written by Richard Addison

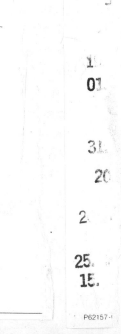

Published by Scholastic Publications Ltd, Marlborough House, Holly Walk, Leamington Spa, Warwickshire CV32 4LS.

© 1987 Scholastic Publications Ltd
Reprinted 1988
Written by Richard Addison
Edited by Jenny Vaughan
Sub-edited by Jackie Cunningham-Craig
Illustrations by Mike Gordon

Printed in Great Britain by
Loxley Brothers Ltd, Sheffield

ISBN 0 590 707000

Front and back cover: Martyn Chillmaid

Contents

4 INTRODUCTION

6 BEGINNER ACTIVITIES
Stop-go   7
Stop-go with instruments   8
Magic stick   8
Play and move   9
Loud and quiet   10
High and low   12
Tuned instrument games   14
Greetings   15
Independence   16
A steady beat   16
Movement in rhythm – 1   18
The echo game   19
Funny voices   20
Doh and Soh and funny noises   20
Doh-Soh-Lah   21
Planning and performing   22
Playing and singing –
By memory and by ear   23
Musical pictures   24
Giant   24

26 INTERMEDIATE ACTIVITIES
Fun with words   27
Follow-my-leader   28
Shakes, bangs and beats   29
High and low, up and down   30
Learning more notes   32
Play by ear   33
Making songs   34
Greetings – the fixed tune   35
Accompanying a song   36
More clapping   36
Make a round – 1   38
Movement in rhythm – 2   39
Build with rhythm   40
Character rhythms   41
Pitch – a wider canvas   42
A musical story   43
Pictures from poems   45

48 ADVANCED ACTIVITIES
Greetings – developments   49

Gesture conducting 50
Semi-sustaining
   instruments 51
Rhythmic backing 52
Composing a song 53
Patchwork with tunes 54
Writing – 1 54
A different set of notes 56
Fun with scales 57
Notes for *The Drunken Sailor*
   and others 58
Atmospherics in sound 59

Action replay 60
Sequence and variation 62
Two tunes at once 64
Writing – 2 65
Chords – experiments 66
Chords – traditional
   practice 67
Chords – reading the
   symbols 68
Making a round – 2 69
Making a music-story
   drama 71

78 RHYME BANK 1

82 RHYME BANK 2

**86 REPRODUCIBLE
MATERIAL**
Graphic notation 87
Rhythms 1 94
Rhythms 2 99
Rhythms 3 108
Songs 112
Lined paper 125
Addison body notation 126
Curwen hand signs 127

Introduction

This book is organised in a 'spiral' pattern of learning. The first part consists of 18 sections, each describing an activity in its simplest form, or dealing with the simplest of musical concepts and skills. All these activities are worth repeating as often as possible. Specific ages are not mentioned, as experience counts for nearly as much as age, but all the activities for this first part have been done over a school year by four- and five-year-olds in an inner city school.

Teachers of older children are advised to start with these early activities and progress through them quickly, rather than plunge straight in with the intermediate activities. The intermediate and advanced activities involve more complicated work and combinations of different concepts, though the type of activities and the way they are organised remain the same.

The aim in organising the classroom for all these activities should be to devolve leadership from the teacher on to the children. All children should have the opportunity to lead and take decisions, for music is like art in that every child must have the opportunity to play with it afresh. When a child is asked to make a decision on a musical matter, the result cannot be *wrong* — it is a matter of choice. We may or may not like this choice, but we cannot describe it as wrong!

There are two objects in giving children the responsibility of musical choice:

- to develop aesthetic awareness;
- to develop their self-confidence and assurance in handling the medium of sound.

Much of the purpose of this book will be lost if a teacher does not frequently relinquish leadership in favour of the children.

This applies more and more as the children grow older. Eight-year-olds, for example, can sometimes be given sessions in which, working in groups of their own choosing, they can do as they please for half an hour. Some may read tunes, others may make up tunes on pipes, while yet others can dance, act and sing. All should work purposefully and perform to the rest of the class at the end of the session. Ten- and eleven-year-olds can be expected to do much more, so long as they have learned to play with a purpose either in the ways suggested in this book or in ways the teacher may devise.

INSTRUMENTS

Most schools have a selection of untuned instruments and, if possible, these should be available for children to use in free or activity time. Home-made instruments are now fairly common. Teachers should encourage children to make items that produce interesting sounds — and to bring potential instruments they make, or come across, into the classroom.

Tuned instruments are extremely important and as many as possible should be available. You can buy small chromatic (ie with black and white bars) glockenspiels for a fraction of the cost of a xylophone, and even six-year-olds can learn to handle them. But of course, good quality xylophones, glockenspiels and metallophones are also very desirable, and electric organs are now cheap enough to fit into a primary school budget.

A tape recorder is a must, and it should be one with an adjustable volume input control for recording. An automatically adjusting input control will completely destroy any build-up or fade-out the children produce in their work.

ACTIVITIES

This book suggests many different types of activity, and it is up to the teacher to balance the hard work ones against those which are more spontaneous. There is one area of activity that really does need regular treatment if good progress is to be made, and that is pitch. Research shows that the best age to develop vocal pitch skills is between four and eight, so we should not waste these precious years.

DEFINITIONS

One or two terms in the text need defining: *Percussion instrument* is used to denote the untuned variety.

Improvise means play spontaneously, without planning or recalling. Most work with younger children will take this form. *Compose* means the opposite of *improvise*. It means planning, remembering and repeating. It does not necessarily mean writing anything down.

RHYME BANKS
Two collections of rhymes are included. The first is very rhythmic in character, and many of the rhymes are nonsense words.

The second contains short poems, with meanings that might lend themselves to particular musical treatments.

Suggestions for the ways these rhymes can be used are included in the text.

REPRODUCIBLE MATERIALS
This includes:

- graphic notation and rhythms, which should be cut out and stuck on to cards in large enough numbers for the children to use;
- three songs for each stage, written in 'words on staff' notation, and arranged for two-part singing with chord symbols;
- wide-lined music paper (not usually available) for children's use, and body and hand signs used for signalling pitch.

Three recommended books:

Make your own Musical Instruments, M Mandell and R E Wood, Blandford Press

Musical Instruments You Can Make, H Garnett, Pitman Publishing

Vibrations, D Sawyer, Cambridge University Press

Beginner activities

Stop-go

Musical aims
To develop the feel of a steady beat, and the sense of 'twice-as-quick'.
To develop quickness of response in the act of starting and stopping in choral/speech.

What you need
The reproducible material on page 100.

What to do
Show the children the 'da-da-da-da-dumm dumm' card (Reproducible material, page 100). Place it on a stand and start chanting it in a fairly quiet speaking voice.
● Beckon to the children to join you, as you say it in a steady rhythm again and again. Gesture to the children to stop.

● Invite a child to come out and signal to you to start and then to stop. Let the child do it several times.
● Invite another child to signal 'Go' and 'Stop' to the whole class. If signals are not clear, and children do not stop or start speaking promptly, discuss the problem with the children and practise all together, making clear signs. Then invite a few more volunteers to lead.
● Finally, divide the class into groups of five or six and appoint the first leader from each group. Let everyone in the group have a turn at leading. All the groups may carry out this activity at the same time, but they will not, of course, all be speaking in unison.

Variation
Instead of using gestures to stop and start the group, use the appropriate rhythm card. When it is visible, the group speaks. When it is hidden or reversed the group is silent.

Stop-go with instruments

Musical aims
To develop the ability to hold an instrument still and soundlessly.
To develop quickness of response in starting to play and stopping.
To develop a feeling for the musical effect of silence contrasted with sound.

What you need
Any percussion instruments. Children will have to do some preliminary work on manipulating these. Make sure they know how either to play each instrument or hold it still. Do not, at this stage, go in for too much subtlety – work on one thing at a time. Tape recorder.

What to do
Use similar gestures to those you used in the previous activity (Stop-go) to start the children playing and to stop them.
● Split the class into two halves and appoint a leader for each. Get these leaders to work with their backs to each other as they start and stop their respective groups, so that they will not follow each other! Tape record a half-minute of this activity and re-play it to the children.
● When you break the class into smaller groups, you can either choose them at random, or you may prefer to group types of instruments – drums and 'clickers' (wood), 'ringers' (triangles, cymbals, bells) and 'shakers' (tambourines, maracas).
● It is advisable to have each group playing alone for at least some of the time, in order to cut down noise level and encourage close listening to the different timbres of each instrument.

Magic stick

Musical aims
To develop control of instruments.
To respond to visual signals.
To develop confidence in playing 'solo'.
To develop musical imagination.

What you need
Any percussion instruments, a drum stick or a conducting stick.

What to do
All children stand in a circle holding their instruments. A leader is appointed and given a drum stick, a conducting

stick or a 'wizard's baton'. This is the magic stick. When it points at an instrument, that instrument has to play. But when it points at another instrument, the first one must stop. In other words, children should only play when pointed at.

• Form smaller groups by dividing the circle into smaller segments of, say, eight children, and have a leader for each segment.

• Encourage the children to make their instruments 'say' really interesting things and insist on quietness when they are not being pointed at.

Play and move

Musical aims
To connect the ideas of music and movement.
To develop musical and movement imagination.
To develop aural and visual responses.

What you need
Easily portable percussion instruments.
Plenty of space will be required.

What to do
It is a good idea to start with a demonstration before getting the children to work in pairs.

• Have all children standing without instruments in their own space. Emphasise that silence means stillness, and that the sound of the teacher's instrument means movement. At first, keep your instrumental playing very simple, concentrating on stopping and starting. Later, develop rapid playing contrasted with slow playing and let that develop into gradual change from fast to slow, as well as sudden change.

• Let the children work in pairs. One leads with the instrument. The other moves 'according to what the instrument says'.

• Demonstrate the complementary procedure – the teacher moves and children play their instruments to suit these movements. Then get the children to work in pairs in this way.

Loud and quiet

Musical aims
To develop the concepts of loud and quiet.
To develop the ability to use the voice, or instruments loudly and quietly.
To develop the ability to discriminate between *loud, louder, quiet* and *quieter* sounds and to appreciate their potential for musical expression.

What you need
Voices and either rhythms from the reproducible material or a rhyme from the first rhyme bank (see pages 78 to 81).

What to do
Introduce the material and make sure the children know it thoroughly. The following suggestions may be helpful, using the rhyme 15:
One, two, three, four
● Chant the words, in a good rhythm.
● Chant the rhyme antiphonally with the class. This means, you say the numbers and they say the words, and then they should say the numbers and you say the words.
● Divide the class into four groups and appoint leaders.
● As soon as their leader points to them, all the members of a group should chant the rhyme together. Meanwhile, you should keep chanting the rhyme continually.
● Next, the leader of each group points to individuals within the group and at that point, only the people pointed at should speak. Again, you should keep on chanting the rhyme continually to keep it going.
● Using the signals illustrated, get one child to signal to you as you speak the rhyme, indicating whether you should be loud or quiet.
● Now get another child to signal loud or quiet, for the whole class.
● Break the class first into two groups, then gradually into smaller ones.

Probable snags

Children may make the signals change too fast. Encourage them to work on a line each, either loud or quiet, to start with.

When two groups are working at the same time, the children in one group will be diverted by hearing the other group. Do not worry about this too much – keep working at the exercise until they become independent.

Variations

Gradually bring in the idea of *getting louder* or *quieter*.

● Use the cards from the Reproducible material (pages 88–90) to indicate *loud* and *quiet* according to the size of the writing. Let groups of children arrange these cards and perform their arrangement.

High and low

Musical aims
To develop the concepts of high and low as applied to the pitch of the voice.
To develop the ability to modulate the voice high and low.
To develop the ability to discriminate high and low sounds and to appreciate children's potential for musical expression.

What you need
Voices,
percussion instruments,
tuned percussion instruments,
piano (if available) and so on.

Discussion
The words *high* and *low* are normally used for meanings other than pitch: 'The bird flew *high* in the air'; 'The plane flew *low* over the houses'; 'The volume is too *low*', 'The volume is too *high*'.

In music *loud* and *quiet* are used to describe volume. It is important to stick to these terms in musical use. Children will need all our help to guide them towards the concept of high and low pitch. This is the foundation of later music reading.

What to do
Hold your hand high in the air and start chanting 'da-da-da-da dumm-dumm' in a very high, squeaky voice.
● Lower your hand suddenly and continue in a low, gruff voice.
● Continue with the usual methods of getting the children

da-da-da-dum.

DA-DA-DA-DUM

to lead and working in smaller groups.
● Use the rhyme *Diddlety, diddlety, dumpty*, on page 80.
Modulate your voice upwards at the words 'up the plum
tree' and down again at the words 'fetch her down'.
● Use the following rhyme for the children to act (in
pairs) and for you and the children to chant as follows:

(High voice) *Little Robin Redbreast sat upon a tree*
(Low voice, rising) *Up went tabby cat*
(High voice, descending) *Down went he*
(High voice, descending) *Down came tabby cat*
(Get faster) *Away Robin ran*
(Squeaky voice) *I'm little Robin Redbreast, catch me if
you can.*

● Get the children to supply appropriate voices for the
story of the *Three Bears*.
● Ask them to respond in movement to high sounds of
your voice and then to low sounds. Start by making the
contrast obvious and gradually ask for more subtle
discrimination.
● Use untuned and/or tuned percussion, and/or the
piano for similar work.
● Using a piano, help the children to find the low notes
(longer strings, on the left) and high notes (shorter ones
on the right). When you talk in a low voice, get the
children to play low notes. When you talk in a high voice
the children are to play high notes.
● Discuss with the children the relative pitch of the
untuned percussion and group them in three groups,
high, medium and low.
● Play the Magic stick or Stop-go games described on
pages 7 and 8.
● Use any of the first collection of rhymes (pages 78–81)
for signalling or leadership games, using up and down
movements of the hand to indicate pitch of voice.

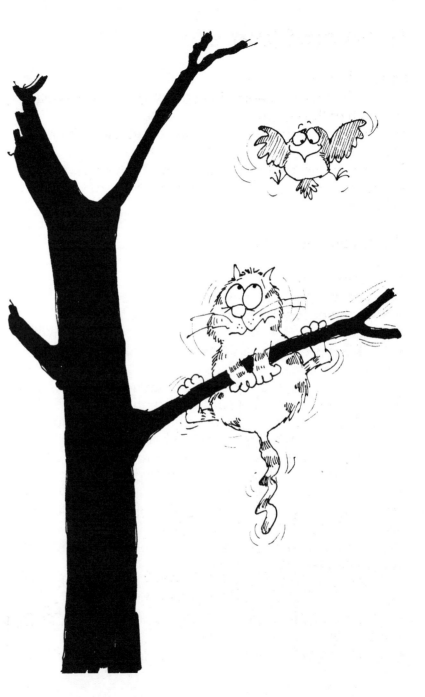

Tuned instrument games

Musical aims
To help children to develop an accurate sense of pitch by letting them hear specific notes repeatedly.
To help children's motor control in handling tuned instruments and fluency in improvising.
To help children to develop a sense of phrasing.

What you need
A large glockenspiel or xylophone or a set of chime bars. At least three beaters.

What to do
Remove all notes except C, D, E, F, G.
- Play the following improvising game:
- Place the glockenspiel on a table in front of you with the low notes on your right as the picture shows. (This will be upside down for you.)
- Play a short phrase of three or four notes.
- The first child plays an answering phrase of a few notes. Play the phrase again, letting a second child play, and so on. The aim is to get smooth follow-on.
- Do not try to plan or remember what you have done, and do not encourage the children to do so.
- When you have repeated the exercise about twice with the whole class, explain that all the notes have 'playing names' (C D E F G) and 'singing names' (*Doh, Ray, Me, Fah, Soh*). For singing, it is easier to learn only one or two notes at a time:
- 'So lets take them all off except for *Doh* (C) *Soh* (G), and then we'll get used to their sound.'
- Continue with the improvising game as before, but with only *Doh* (C) and *Soh* (G).
- Using one of the rhymes from the first bank, that the

children already know, play and say a line of the rhyme and let each child play and say the next, and so on. Again, do not pause, and remember to repeat lines. The aim is fluency.
- Both these examples can be done in groups, provided enough instruments are available.
- Copying games should be played as a contrast to improvising games. One child plays – and repeats – a very short tune (still using the two notes). You play the same tune back. Later another child can do the copying.
- Instrumental signals for various routine instructions can be worked out: eg 'time for your milk' could be G C C G. The children will soon learn them!

Greetings

Musical aims
To help children to pitch their voices accurately.
To get them to associate singing with happiness and warm feelings.

What you need
Voices,
A glockenspiel for reference.

What to do
At the start of the day, appoint a child to play the glockenspiel with the singers, and whenever you request this.

● Start singing, eg:
'Good morning Jane
Doh Doh Doh Soh.'
Jane sings back:
'Good morning Mr(s) So-and-so
Doh Doh Doh Doh Soh Soh Soh.'
● Use real names, of course.
● Continue this with all the children in the class. Many will not reply in tune, and you should ignore this for several days, until they are all replying unselfconsciously. Then, ask the 'untuned' singer to listen as you sing the tune and after that, get the other children to 'help out'.
● When a previously untuned singer first sings in tune, make your pleasure known. Everyone should be successful within a few weeks.
● The next stage – and there is no hurry – is for the children to reverse your tune. This means that you sing:
'Good morning Jane
Doh Doh Doh Soh.'
She replies: *'Good morning Mr(s) So-and-So*
Soh Soh Soh Soh Soh Doh Doh Doh.'

● You could introduce this idea of reversal in a humorous way by inventing short rhymes about each child, eg:
'Good morning Jane, walking down the lane
Doh Doh Doh Soh Soh Soh Soh Soh Soh Doh;
Good morning Mike – riding on your bike.'
● Some names may prove more difficult to rhyme!

Independence

Musical aims
To help children to gain musical independence.
To prepare them for singing rounds.
To reinforce the children's ability both to memorise and to speak rhymes.

What you need
Any of the rhymes from the first rhyme bank (see pages 78–81).
Any of the rhythms from reproducible material (see pages 94–111).

What to do
Select a rhyme, say, *Rub a dub dub (see page 79)*. Clap a steady beat and chant it rhythmically to the class.
- Get them to join in with some rhythmic movement in time with your clapping. Make sure they all learn the rhyme fluently.
- Ask the class to turn their backs to you.
- Let them start chanting the rhyme all together, with your help. Then, you should start at the beginning when they are saying 'who do you think they be'. Challenge them not to let you put them off.
- Develop this game. Instead of saying the rhyme in round with them, say one of the triple rhythms from the reproducible material (see page 108).
- Say the rhyme in a louder voice.
- Let the class face you as you chant the rhyme in round, but avoid eye contact.
- Deliberately stare at various children as you chant the rhyme in round. Challenge these children not to be put off.
- Divide the class in half, and let the two groups chant the rhyme in round. Later, have four groups.

A steady beat

Musical aims
To help children to keep a steady pulse beat independent of the rhythms of the words or song.
To help them to relate to each other and become inter-dependent.

What you need
Hands and voices.
Rhymes, rhythms, or songs.

What to do
Keeping a steady beat in music is a most important accomplishment and requires considerable independence.
- Choose a child who has a fair rhythmic sense and clap with him or her as follows:
- First beat: each others' hands;
- Second beat: your own hands.

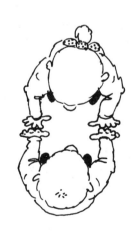 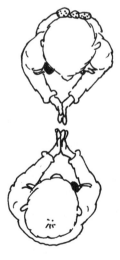

- Let all the class count *one-two-one-two* etc as you clap.
- Let all children pair up and do the same as you count with them. Some pairs may be so good at this that they go twice as fast as everyone else! Slow them down.
- Stand the children in two lines as illustrated.

illustrated) and to be able to clap the beat whilst chanting rhymes or rhythms or singing songs.
- You will find this may take time to achieve but children love it and will probably take it into the playground with them.

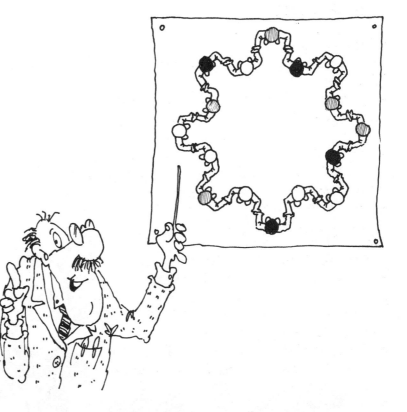

- Count with them as they all try to keep together. Make sure they clap the other person's hands on the first beat.
- When it is all going well, (and this may not be until the third or fourth attempt) try chanting a rhyme as they continue counting. Soon some will join you but others may find they lose their clapping beat. Persevere.
- The final stage is to make a big double circle (as

Variation
When all children have a feel for the steady beat, let them in pairs work out other movements that represent a steady beat. Ask them to work out a movement that involves both of them.

Movement in rhythm—1

Musical aims
To reinforce rhythm patterns with body movement.
To develop movement imagination.

What you need
Voices.
A few instruments if you wish.
4/4 rhythm from rhythm bank (see pages 94–111).

What to do
Select a 4/4 rhythm from the rhythm bank and chant it
with all the class over and over again. Have some
children play the instruments if you like. Ask all the
children to invent movements for the rhythm. Ask each
one to do a movement different from anybody else's.

Variation 1
Stop occasionally. Ask one child to perform his
movement for everyone else to copy. Then go back to
individual movements.

Variation 2
Ask everyone to do one movement. One child plays a
drum – perhaps with your help. When the drum is played
louder, the movement gets bigger and vice versa.
Change the rhythm occasionally.

The echo game

Musical aims
To develop short-term memory for musical phrases.
To further develop the loud-quiet concept.
To promote independent action.
To develop visual-aural awareness and understanding.

What you need
Voices and instruments.
Rhythm cards (see pages 94–111).

What to do
Choose about four rhythm cards (you can use fewer or more, depending on experience) from the rhythm bank – all duples or all triples.
● Use these cards yourself to start with and place them where only you can see them. Clap a steady beat and chant one of the rhythms. Get the class to echo you at once. Repeat as often as necessary to get a really accurate response. Go straight on, without any break in the beat, to another rhythm. Continue as before.

Variation 1
Sing the rhythm to a definite tune and get the class to copy you.

Variation 2
Chant the rhythm and get the class to chant it back. Then get everyone to play it on instruments.

Variation 3
Chant the rhythm with big variations in volume and then get the class to echo using their voices, then instruments.

Variation 4
As 3, but have the class do the opposite to what you do: ie answer loud with quiet and vice versa.

Continuation
Place one of the rhythm cards where everyone can see it. Chant it, pointing at the notes. Get everyone to copy this.
● Place another card, as dissimilar as possible, beside it and do the same.
● Chant one of the cards and ask children which one it was. Get individual children to read the cards aloud instead of you. The class should echo each one.

Development
Increase the number of cards you use. Split the class into smaller groups.

Note: Do not try to teach any theory at this stage. Just ensure that the children associate the different sounds with the appropriate symbols.

Funny voices

Musical aims
To develop flexibility in the use of the voice and to help children to realise its possibilities.

What you need
Voices.
Rhymes from first rhyme bank (see pages 78–81).

What to do
Choose one of the meaningless rhymes from the first rhyme bank and get the children to learn it thoroughly, in the usual way.
● Chant it all together and ask children to use 'funny voices'. (If the children are very inhibited and you cannot get them to do this, you may have to give some examples!)
● Ask individuals to demonstrate their funny voice and get everyone to copy it.
● Select about four funny voices and ask for suggestions for a signal (in the form of movement) for each.
● Get one child to signal the different funny voices as everyone chants the rhyme, using the voices as instructed, by the child signalling.
● Include in the voices a *singing* voice, and get the children to decide on another signal for that. Incorporate this into the activity.

Note: This is simply to develop the children's understanding and feel for a *singing* as opposed to a *speaking* voice. It is the failure to differentiate that characterises the 'untuned' singers – who are usually boys. At this early stage, do not worry about specific notes.

Doh and Soh and funny noises

Musical aims
To help children to pitch their voices accurately.
To help them keep accurately pitched notes in mind, and reproduce them.

What you need
Voices.
Body or hand signals (see pages 126 and 127).
With young children, puppets may be used
A glockenspiel, xylophone, or chime bars, using notes C and G only.

What to do
Before introducing the notes ask the children to suggest funny noises. Select about three of these and ask for suggestions for a body signal for each one. Get a child to signal these funny noises for everyone to respond to.
● Now introduce *Doh*. Sing it firmly with an instrumental note, firstly to reinforce it and then as another sound, using the appropriate signal for it. Continue, letting individual children lead using both funny noises and *Doh*. Then add *Soh*.

Doggie Doh

Silly Soh

Doh-Soh-Lah

Musical aims

To increase pitch discrimination and vocal ability.
To make more interesting melodies.
To get children to make the connection between 'real' music and their own note learning.

What you need

Voices.
Tuned instruments.

What to do

Repeat the activities Tuned instrument games (page 14); Greetings (page 15) and Doh and Soh and funny noises (page 20), in all cases using three notes instead of two.
● Work on 'little tunes'. Get a child to signal a small group of notes – perhaps just three. Do not sing them. Ask the child to repeat the signal twice and then get everyone to sing this 'little tune', signalling as they sing.

Note: Keep this as a whole-class activity for quite a time, as you will need to help the children to remember and repeat their signals and also to sing the right notes.
● Signal to the class the first seven notes of Twinkle, Twinkle, Little Star (Doh Doh Soh Soh Lah Lah Soh). Repeat this several times and ask the children to guess what the tune is.
● Signal the first four notes of Lavender's Blue: Doh Soh Soh Soh. (Note: It is of course necessary for the children to be familiar with these tunes prior to doing this activity).
● Follow this by singing the next four notes, without words: pom pom pom pom.
● Continue, signalling only: Doh Lah Lah Lah.
● When the children have guessed the tune, signal and

sing it together as follows:
● (Signal) Doh Soh Soh Soh (sing) Dilly Dilly, (Signal) Doh Lah Lah Lah –
● (Signal) Doh Soh Soh Soh (sing) Dilly, Dilly, you shall be queen.
● Next time, one or several children could play the second and third lines, with or without the Dilly Dilly's.

Planning and performing

Musical aims
To help children feel the process of composition.
To give them pride of achievement.
To develop concentration and memory.

What you need
Voices and instruments. A rhythm from pages 94–111.

What to do
Almost all the activities so far suggested can lead to the planning and performing of short 'pieces'. Here is a suggestion for one particular activity.
● Take one of the rhythms from the rhythm bank. Get the children to say it, play it, move to it and sing it.
● Ask a child: 'How many times would you like us to perform it?
● Write the answer on the blackboard – say the child suggested 'seven': 1 2 3 4 5 6 7

● Divide the class into speakers, players, movers, singers (according to their choice).
● Ask for decisions on who performs at each repetition.

● Invent diagrams to describe each – say:

● Your final picture may look like this:

● Instead of a picture diagram you could memorise it, gradually extending it from the beginning as suggestions are made or you could appoint a child to lead each group and perform at the appropriate place.

Playing and singing – by memory and by ear

Musical aims
To develop children's skills in relating pitched sounds to instrumental notes.

What you need
Voices, tuned instruments.

What to do
Using the notes *Doh, Soh* and *Lah* only, sing a very short phrase and ask one child or more to play it after you and with you. A tactful way of asking a child to do this could be something like: 'John, will you see if I sang it right?'
● As children develop in pitch skill themselves, they will be able to do this easily, but until they reach this stage, let

them try to check themselves or each other as above.
● For the following activity use only *Doh* and *Soh* to start with, but add *Lah* when you feel it is appropriate. (Even *Doh* by itself can be used, for the purpose of rhythmic memorising.)
● Play the two notes to the children and ask them to turn their backs. Now play a phrase of only three notes. Play it again, then ask for volunteers to play it back to you. (Everyone will be quite sure they remember the tune!). The first person to play it correctly plays the next three note tune, repeats it and chooses the next child to play it back and so on.
● You may find the children are *very* keen on this activity even if they are unsuccessful at first.

23

Musical pictures

Musical aims
To develop a sense of imagery in terms of sound.
To help them to work together purposefully.

What you need
Tuned instruments.

What to do
Composers sometimes use visual images – as Beethoven did for example, in his *Pastoral Symphony*. Such imagery is not essential to creative music, but children do find it stimulating.
- Since movement is music's closest relation, things or creatures in motion provide good images. Ask one group of children to make a sound to suggest an animal moving, and then get the others to try to guess the animal. For a human being moving, you could choose walking, running, skipping, on a floor, through leaves, coming closer, going away . . . and so on. For machinery, try a bulldozer, a mechanical toy, starting up, slowing down, or a car changing gear. For natural movement, choose falling leaves, rain-drops, the wind blowing, lightning flashing and so on.
- Mood is another great stimulus for music. Ask the children, together or in small groups, to play happy, sad or angry music, gentle, surprising, jerky or smooth music.
- Music may also be used to illustrate stories or poems. Choose a well-known story, discuss which instruments suit which characters and which events and moods could be illustrated with which background sounds. Then tell the story and let the children add the music spontaneously, repeating the event with slight improvements on future occasions.

A music-movement-drama project

Giant – by Clive Sansom

Musical aim
To stimulate and encourage children in multi-media activity.

What you need
Instruments of all types.

The poem
The tall, stern Giant moves
With long, strong, even strides
(Every little boy who sees him
Runs away and hides)

The Giant, angry, grumpy, surly
Marches over house and hill
(Every little boy is hiding
Very quiet and still)

On the Giant trudges, glumly
Gruff and grim he takes his way
(All the little boys are happy
Out they come to play)

Clive Sansom

What to do

Say the rhyme many times with the children, encouraging them to move as the rhyme suggests. Exaggerate the slowness of the giant by using a slow and deep voice and use a light, quick voice for the little boys.

- Divide the class into two halves. Let one half be the movers, whilst the others improvise on percussion instruments. Discuss suitable instruments with the children, for both the giant and child music.
- Ask for child volunteers to improvise tunes and gradually to develop and remember a tune.
- Now divide the class into four groups. One group forms the musicians, another is the giant, the remainder are the children. Perform it with actions four times, so that every child plays every part.

Intermediate activities

Fun with words

Musical aims
To find rhythmic feeling in words.
To help children to keep a good ensemble.
To develop independence in musical ensemble.

What you need
Voices, percussion instruments.

What to do
Ask children to think of the name of one of their most popular television programmes, toy, food, or hobby. Write the names they suggest on the blackboard, saying them as you write.

● Take an instrument and tap out the rhythm of one of the names. Ask children which one it was. (Do it several times before you give the answer.)

● Ask a child to tap out another name and get everyone else to guess which it was. And so on.

● Now get the children to 'pair clap' in two-beat claps (see A steady beat, pages 16 and 17) and ask each pair of children to chant one of the names on the blackboard as they clap. Beat a drum to keep them clapping together.

● Stop them and tell them to keep changing the volume (loudness) of their chanting. Next, stop them and tell them to keep changing the *pitch* (high/low) of their chanting. Next let them work in pairs, one with an instrument and one with the voice.

● Ask them to chant and play their words alternately. Keep beating your own drum steadily and move around the children, trying to keep them with you.

● Now let them add to their chants. Suppose they were chanting *EastEnders*. Now they will chant *We like East Enders best of all.*

● Let them listen to and guess each others favourite programmes by hearing the lengthened version.

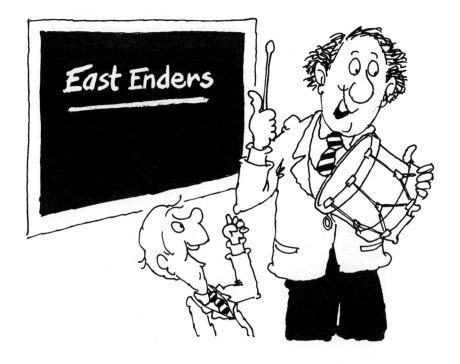

Follow-my-leader

Musical aims
To develop children's understanding of the importance of timing in music.
To improve leadership competence.

What you need
Voices, percussion instruments.
Rhymes from first rhyme bank (see pages 78–81).

What to do
Choose one of the longer rhymes from the first rhyme bank such as *One, two, buckle my shoe, Chick, chick, chatterman,* and *Intery, mintery, cutery corn.*
• Let the children get to know the rhyme thoroughly. (See *Loud and quiet* page 10.)

• Give a demonstration. With your hands poised in the air, start the children chanting the rhyme as you beat time like a real conductor. Stop the children occasionally by holding your hands quite still, and then start again. Speed up sometimes, slow down at other times (but not too abruptly) and stop sometimes.
• Hand over to a child. You will find that some children have considerable ability, while others have less. Let the more successful leaders have further scope by dividing the class into two, three or four groups. Let the conductor indicate which group is to chant by looking and turning in their direction. This means he is indicating speed, stop-start, and which group should play, all at the same time.

Variation
Let some or all of the children play and say the rhyme on percussion instruments. These may be grouped at random or according to their tone colours. Let each conductor, signalling as described above, have two or three turns in order to get more precise timing — especially in exact starts. This is an excellent discipline for players as well as conductors and yet it is great fun.

Note: Some children will play the actual rhythm of the words, whereas some will play the background beat. A few may play neither! Ignore this and concentrate on speeding up, slowing down, starting and stopping together.

Shakes, bangs and beats

Musical aims

To improve control of musical instruments.
To increase children's understanding of the dramatic meanings of musical sounds.
To help children to be decisive in leadership.

What you need

Percussion instruments, tape recorder.

What to do

Demonstrate movements to indicate *shakes* (let your hands shake in the air) and *bangs* (one fist bangs on to the other open hand).
- *Loudness* is indicated by large movements – shakes or bangs.
- *Quietness* is indicated by small movements, *silence* by no movement.
- Let the children conduct.
- Divide the class into two, with a conductor for each. Both groups can operate at once. If you divide the children into smaller groups it will be as well to give each group a short turn while the others listen.
- Tape record, play back and discuss with the class at each stage.

Developments

Beats can be shown by a series of regular bangs. Players can be encouraged to play *da-das* as well as the beats (*dumms*).
- Movement can be brought into the picture. Half the class may be the band with its own conductor. The other half may be the movers who respond to the sounds of the band. Make sure that loudness is reflected in big movements and quietness by small ones. The class may work in pairs. The conductor of each pair is now encouraged to indicate bangs, shakes and steady beats with the whole body (not necessarily all at once!) instead of with just the hands.
- Use the appropriate card graphics from the reproducible material, or material written by the children themselves to make, practise and perform short pieces either in music or in music and movement. Record them, play them back and discuss them.

High and low, up and down

Musical aims
To develop further the high/low concept as applied to musical pitch.
To further develop musical imagination.

What you need
Good quality glockenspiel, xylophone or piano, voices, rhymes from first rhyme bank (See pages 78–81).

What to do
To begin with do the playing yourself and get the children to move. Use two types of sound only to start with – those used in the previous activity. Use them on low or high notes and ask the children to respond with movements near the ground or high in the air. Do not concern yourself with loud or quiet at present, but speed can feature, as the children will respond naturally (shakes on xylophones are executed by rapidly stroking two or three notes).
● A few children can also take turns at playing, following your example. Group work is possible only if you have enough good quality instruments.

Variations
Play hunt-the-thimble, using sounds. The higher the sounds the nearer the finder is to the object being hunted. Only two can play, but non-playing children can copy the instrument with their voices.
● Use a nonsense rhyme from the first rhyme bank. When children have learned it thoroughly, ask one of them to indicate pitch by means of low-high hand movements. Make sure movements are not too quick, but let them include the gradations between highest and lowest notes.

Developments
This development requires concentration on two concepts at once. As these two are the very ones that are usually confused, approach the activity gently and persevere with it. Do the signalling yourself to start with.
●Use the nonsense rhyme you used above and use both hands for signalling. For low and quiet notes have the hands together, low down.
●For low and loud phrases, have the hands apart, low down.
●For high and quiet phrases, have the hands together, high above your head.

- For high and loud phrases, have the hands apart, high above your head.
- Do not alter more than one thing at a time. Do not change from one signal to another except at the change of line.
- Stick to one signal, until everyone (or nearly everyone) is doing it correctly.
- Gradually encourage the children to signal. They must learn to be sensitive to the capabilities of the other children and to the possibilities of the rhyme.
- Persevere, and gradually divide the class into smaller groups, each with its own rota of leaders.

Learning more notes

Musical aims
To develop further children's sense of pitch relationships, letting them play and hear specific notes.
To improve further their motor control in handling pitched instruments.

What you need
Xylophones, glockenspiels, chime bars – as many are as available. Rhythm cards (See pages 94-111).

What to do
Use a glockenspiel with some of the notes removed, as described in Tuned instrument games on page 14. Use the notes *Doh Me Soh Lah* to play the improvising game
C   E   G   A
outlined there, in which you play a short phrase and children improvise answering phrases.

●Similarly, you can play the game using rhymes, as described in the same activity. This involves playing and singing a line of a rhyme taken from the first rhyme bank. The children answer this by playing and singing the next line, and so on. This time, use a rhyme with a more complicated rhythm, preferably the 6/8 type.
●*Still working through Tuned instrument games, play the copying game described there, in which one child plays and repeats a short tune, and another child plays it back.*
●Using rhythm cards (6/8 or 4/4) get the children to improvise (not to try to remember) tunes to fit the rhythm. Depending on the competence of the children, they can use a one-bar rhythm or a two-bar rhythm. They must remember and repeat the rhythm, but not the notes of their improvised melodies.

Note: There is a very important musical reason for this game. It is a compositional feature or trick of many composers to use a repeated rhythm whilst varying the melody used with it. Listen to the famous *Blue Danube* tune by Johann Strauss and count how many times he uses the initial rhythm.

dumm   dumm dumm dumm   dumm (hoooo) dumm   dumm (hoooo) dumm dumm (hoooo)

● Play it to the children. Note that Strauss never repeats the melody of any phrase. Many similar examples occur in songs, such as *What shall we do with the Drunken Sailor?* – in which the repeated words are set to different phrases of melody.
● As a development of this game, children working in groups of four may each compose one phrase of melody for the same rhythm and then put all four phrases together in whichever order they choose.

Play by ear

Musical aims
To help children to relate the pitched sounds they have learned to existing music.

What you need
Tuned instruments.

What to do
There are several tunes that use *Doh, Me, Soh* and *Lah*, prominently. You can use them in two ways.

Michael row the boat ashore,
Doh Me Soh Me Soh Lah Soh,
Al le lu ya
Me Soh Lah Soh

Cum by a my Lord Cum by a ...
Doh Me Soh Soh Soh Lah Lah Soh

Did you ev er see a lass ie
Doh Me Soh Lah Soh (Fah) Me Doh

- See if the children can discriminate between them when you signal them – in the correct rhythm of course.
- Sing a small piece of one of the tunes using singing names. Ask a child to play it and see if anyone can tell you which tune it comes from.
- Play any of the tunes, or get a child to do so, using the wrong rhythm. See if anyone recognises it.

Making songs

Musical aims
To improve the quality of children's musical imagination both rhythmic and melodic.
To improve short and long term musical memory.

What you need
Rhymes, proverbs etc. Tape recorder.

What to do
Take a simple phrase of words – proverbs are convenient, eg *Make hay while the sun shines*.
● Talk about the actual meaning and the symbolic meaning – giving and receiving plenty of examples.
● Suggest that the children improvise tunes for it. Use singing voices and get everyone to sing it together many times.
● Ask them to use high voices, low voices and tunes involving high and low notes. (The aim is to get children to use their voices to improvise with. It is not to establish a fixed tune at this stage.)
● Now discuss the rhythm and explain that there is a natural way to say these words, but that when you are making a song part of the fun is to change the rhythm. For example, the proverb could run: *make hay – – – while the sun shines*, or *make hay while – – – the sun – – shines – –* or *make – – hay – – – while the sun shines*.
● Ask the children to invent as many different ways of saying the proverb as they can. To avoid self-consciousness let them start off working in pairs. They may clap with their partner as they chant.
● Choose more proverbs and let each pair of children make first a rhythm, and then a rhythm and tune.
● Go round quickly with a tape recorder holding it near to each pair for if you ask each pair to perform aloud to

the others they will forget their own song as they hear everyone else's!

Note: Do not restrict them to only the notes they have learned. Let them be unselfconscious about this. The aim is to develop musical imagination!

Greetings: the 'fixed tune'

Musical aims
To develop further aural/vocal skill and memory for melody.
To develop further musical imagination especially in pitch.

What you need
Voices, using notes *Doh Me Soh Lah*.
A tuned instrument as a guide and check.

What to do
This activity needs to go along hand-in-hand with Greetings on page 15, Doh and Soh and funny noises on page 20 and *Doh-Soh-Lah* on page 21.
● Regularly use hand or body signals to get children reading the signals and singing their own little tunes. When a child has signalled and repeated a little tune and the class has sung it, ask the composer how many times he or she would like it sung.
● Continue by asking one of the following questions:
● 'How shall we sing each time – loudly or quietly?'
● 'Who shall we ask to sing each time?'
● Possible groupings in answer to this last question could be individuals, groups, boys, or girls, or older or younger children.

Greetings – two developments
Sing 'Good morning ————' using any notes. Each child responds with a fixed tune which will need to be learned in advance.

Note: The teacher can help in a subtle way here. Some children will have no difficulty in remembering the fixed tune. In fact it is fairly natural for them to copy each other

in their response. But others who are less pitch-competent may not be able to find the first note of the fixed tune. If your phrase ends with the first note of the fixed tune they will find it much easier.
● Then, sing a 'fixed tune' as you greet each child. They should each respond with any tune, but not the fixed tune. If a child is singing slightly out of tune let him or her try again.
● If he or she is very out of tune ask everyone to help. Don't forget to express your pleasure at tunefulness – especially when a child produces it for the first time!

Note: it is important in the greetings games to stick to one type of game for about a week or more, so that practice makes perfect and confidence grows. The more competent the children become, the more a teacher can change the activities around.

Accompanying a song

Musical aims
To help children to be more aware of meaning in a song.
To help children be more aware of form in a song.

What you need
Percussion instruments and voices.

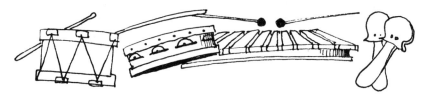

What to do
Listen to and learn *When I was a Little Boy*. (See the Reproducible material page 116).

Ask the children if there are any words which could be illustrated with a sound effect. Try it through. (Examples might be *wheelbarrow, fall, down went the barrow*).

Look at the refrain and split it up as follows (singing):

Group 1 – *to my wing wong waddle*
Group 2 – *to my Jack Straw straddle*
Group 3 – *to my John Fair faddle*
All – *to my long ways home*

● Get a child to point at which group is to sing which phrase. Let other children have a turn.
● Let half the children join in the refrain with their percussion instruments.
● Divide the instruments in three groups. Let one child conduct the instruments as in High and low, up and down, page 30.

More clapping

Musical aims
To establish and reinforce body rhythms in groups of three and four.
To establish the feeling for musical bars.

Note: The bar in music is largely a writing device to make reading easier. It is also however a feeling of accentuation, which is felt on the first beat in every two, three or four beats. Thus the clapping of these 'bars' establishes the whole feeling for musical pulse and accentuation and makes the written symbol easier to understand.

What you need
Voices and/or instruments.

What to do
Follow exactly the same procedures as in *A steady beat* on page 16, but the clapping patterns will be as follows:
For threes:
Beat 1 – clap partner's hands.
Beat 2 – clap own hands.
Beat 3 – clap own knees.
For fours:
Beat 1 – clap partner's right hand.
Beat 2 – clap own hands together.
Beat 3 – clap partner's left hand.
Beat 4 – clap own hands together.

● Clapping in fours, when done in the double circle, is hard to achieve because everyone depends on everyone else. But persevere, as it is popular and well worth the effort.

● The claps can be accompanied by instruments playing one or two rhythms from the cards, by songs or by children improvising on instruments.

● Three-beat songs are rarer than two- or four-beat ones. Here are a few:

There's a hole in my bucket dear
3   1 2 3 1   2 3

Liz a dear Liz a
1 2 3   1 2

The Holly and the ivy when they are both full grown
3 1   2   3 12 3 1   2   3 1 2

Oh my dar-ling oh my dar-ling oh my dar-ling
3   1 2 3   1 2 3   1 2

Clementine
3   1 2

Make a round – 1

Musical aims
To increase independence and security of pitch in singing.
To improve children's ability to sing in parts independently.

What you need
Tuned instruments using notes *Doh Me So Lah*
                          C E G A

The rhyme: Solomon Grundy
Solomon Grundy,
Born on Monday,
Christened on Tuesday,
Married on Wednesday,
Ill on Thursday,
Worse on Friday,
Died on Saturday,
Buried on Sunday,
That was the end of
Solomon Grundy.

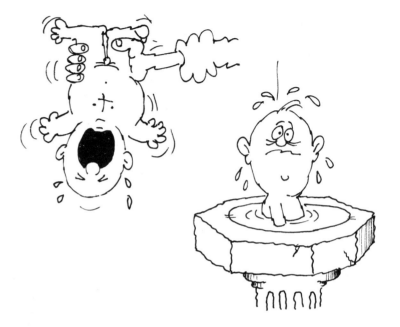

What to do
Let the children learn the rhyme thoroughly using the usual strategies (see Loud and quiet, page 10). It may be better to do this on two or three separate occasions.
● Improvise instrumentally with the children, using the notes given above (see Tuned instrument games, page 14).
● Get the children to signal improvisations and little tunes for a few minutes – one child at a time, signalling to you and the whole class with one or two children playing the tuned instruments.
● Now ask one child to sing a tune for the first line only of the rhyme. Echo it – and get the whole class to do this.

(Tape it if your own memory is not too reliable!)
● Continue with another child doing the second line and so on. Always start each time at the beginning.
● You will probably find that a simple kind of chant emerges with plenty of repetition. Get children to learn it thoroughly.
● To turn this into a canon or round, have the children stand in two circles, facing inwards. Each circle should be as far from the other as possible. Start the first circle singing from the beginning, and let the second circle start when the first one has reached line 2.
● This may not be immediately successful, but it is well worth practising and is a very popular and challenging activity.

Movement in rhythm – 2

Musical aims
To improve children's bodily control of rhythm. To develop co-operation and movement imagination.

What you need
Voices, and perhaps a few instruments.

What to do
As for Movement in rhythm, page 18, but use three-beat rhythms or 6/8 rhythms (the latter not too fast).
● After doing all the steps listed there get the children to work in pairs, doing a co-operative movement of some kind. You could suggest they are some part of a machine. Work also on getting bigger (louder), getting smaller (quieter), getting faster, getting slower.

Build with rhythm

Musical aims

To establish the link between visual symbols of rhythm and their matching sounds.

To demonstrate the use of notation for creative purpose.

To let children experience one of the processes of composition and arrangement.

What you need

Four rhythm cards (see pages 94–111).

Four instruments.

What to do

Use some of the four rhythm cards for practice in reading (see The echo game, page 19). Ask children to choose one (or two if they are capable enough) of the cards.

● Chant the rhythm shown there together several times, using signals for loud and quiet or high and low.

● Ask the class to wait for one beat or for two beats between repetitions. Try both versions many times. Take a vote to find the most popular one: no rests, one beat rest, two beats rest.

● You now have your material to work with; something like this, perhaps:

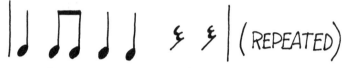

● By questions, make your plan, practise as you go along and if you like write a plan on the blackboard. 'Now, we can chant it play it or sing it. Which shall we do? How many times?'

● 'Shall we play, sing or chant it, or will it be a combination? Shall we chant loudly or quietly?'

● Tape record the result, and you can then use it for movement.

Character rhythms

Musical aims
To help children develop rhythmic imagination.
To help them to use music to portray mood and feeling.

What you need
Percussion instruments.

Introductory note
Just as in Making songs, page 34, the children were asked to sing unselfconsciously, without thinking of the notes they were using, so now we ask them to invent interesting rhythms, without worrying about what these might look like. A rhythm is formed like a pattern on wallpaper, by repetition. So any group of notes, if repeated, becomes a pattern. It may or may not be possible to find a beat, but do not worry about that.

What to do
Ask children for suggestions for rhythms to portray (for instance) anger, sweetness, fun and laughter, surprise, calm and rest, determination.

● When each child offers a rhythm, try to copy it at once. (Use a tape recorder if you don't trust your memory!). Then get everyone to play it a few times. Some children might well like to move, in the appropriate mood.

● Get children to work in pairs, using opposites for their rhythms. For example, they could try a jerky rhythm and a smooth one, or a funny rhythm and a sad one.

● Let them choose suitable instruments and work individually until they know their rhythm. Then let them combine in pairs and adjust the rhythm as they think fit. They can play alternately or they can play together.

● It is most important to accept and enjoy what they do, even if you have doubts about how 'good' it is. Your task as listener and guide is to make sure they do what they intended to do. Give them another chance if they did not, and let them hear themselves on tape. Encourage them to repeat many times.

● Tuned instruments or voices may be added but make sure the children add to the feeling of the piece they have created.

Pitch – a wider canvas

Musical aims
To extend the children's understanding of pitch and to help them hear the same notes in different contexts.

What you need
Tuned instruments.

Introductory note
Set the notes in the following way:
Soh Lah Doh Ray Me
   D   E   G   A   B

Firstly, you will notice that *Ray* has been added to the notes already used.
* This is to prepare the children's ears for another note, so that when they use it for their signalling games it will already be familiar.
* Secondly you will notice that *Doh* is not the lowest note, but lies in the middle. It is important that this should be so sometimes, because it is the case with many songs, of which *Old Macdonald* and *Tom Dooley* are well-known examples. The five notes now introduced (*Doh Ray Me Soh Lah*) form the *Pentatonic* scale (five-tone scale). Many tunes from all over the world use only the notes of this scale. Among the most familiar are many

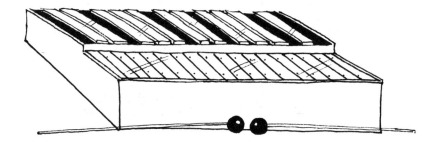

negro spirituals and Scottish tunes (eg *Auld Lang Syne*).

What to do
Explain to the children what you are doing. Play the usual improvisation and copying games to get them familiar with the new pattern of notes.
* Tell them they are all going to learn to play *Old Macdonald had a farm*, that it uses the same notes that they have just been playing and that the first note is G:

Old Macdonald had a farm,
Eee i ee i o,
And on that farm he had some ducks,
Eee i ee i o,
With a quack-quack here, and a quack-quack there,
Here a quack, there a quack, everywhere a quack-quack
Old Macdonald had a farm.

● Let them spend a few minutes trying to work out the first bit of the song. Some will succeed and some will look defeated.
● Ask them about tune to the words: *Here a quack, there a quack, everywhere a quack-quack* (line 6). This is all on one note – G. Make sure that everyone learns to play it, and then sing all of the first verse, letting everyone join in on instruments for that line only.

Now let them try to play:
Eee i ee i o.
B   BA AG
● Give them the first B. Many will succeed, so let them show the others. Then play and sing the verse again, with everyone joining in these two lines.

Add line 5:
With a quack-quack here and a quack-quack there
D   DG   G   G D DG   G   G
Then line 1:
Old Macdonald had a farm
G   G   G D E   ED
Finally, add line 3:
and on that farm he had some ducks
D G G   G   D E E   D
● By the end of each session, you can expect a few children to play lines 1 and 3, a few more to play line 5 and most of the children to play lines 2, 4 and 6. But when performed, every child can join in with some of it. Beginner recorder players may also take part.

A musical story—1

Musical aims
To encourage children to draw upon their sense of imagery in composing music by futher developing their senses of mood, movement and character.

What you need
Voices.
Instruments of all types.

What to do
This is a continuation of the idea of Musical pictures, see page 24.
● As children get older, they can make their illustrations more definitely musical, rather than just sound effects.
● It is best to keep the ideas simple. Encourage older children to do a musical story for the younger ones.
● A very simple story would be Aesops' story of the *Hare and the Tortoise.*

● The story has to be retold so that the music can fit in suitably. It might, therefore, begin:

A hare was entertaining the other animals by boasting of his great speed and agility.

● Follow either with some character music, based on the kind of character rhythms discussed in the previous activity (Character rhythms on page 41), or a boasting song – in which case, encourage the children to keep the words very simple and repetitive, after the style of:

Have you seen the Muffin man
The Muffin man, the Muffin man?
Have you seen the Muffin man
Who lives down Drury Lane?

A parallel in this case might be:

I can run like the wind,
Like the wind, like the wind.
I can run like the wind,
And no one can catch me.

● Many songs use a similar form (*John Brown's body, Skip to my Lou, Here we go round the mulberry bush* etc) and no rhyming is involved.

● Continue with:

Amongst his listeners was Mr Tortoise, a wise old animal who didn't say much.

● Follow with some character music for the tortoise.

● And so the story may be continued with, perhaps, a song for the animal who proposes the race, with a chorus from the other animals.

● For the race itself describe the Tortoise plodding on endlessly, as the Hare stops frequently for a nibble or a sleep.

● The end could be a welcoming chorus from the other animals for the winner, with a middle section that teases the hare, followed by a return to the welcoming chorus.

● The music can be made in many different ways, depending upon how you organise your class. You could work with the whole class, getting decisions from them all the time. Or, if your children are mature enough to work in groups, four groups could each do one of the tasks, either all together or at different times.

● When complete, the story could be taped and played to another class, or performed live and even acted.

Pictures from poems

Musical aims
To help children develop a feeling response to poetry.
To express this in musical terms.

What to do
No definite procedure can be established for this work.
Some poems lend themselves to singing, some do not.
- Musical ideas, suggested by ideas in the words, can accompany the words or can be performed in silent periods between sections of the words.
- The words may be spoken or sung by one child or by everyone. They may even be omitted altogether and used as an inspiration for a picture in music.
- The poems that follow were all written by children of primary age and are chosen for their use of imagery. Your own children will probably produce similar examples.

The Waterfall
The water from the rushing falls,
Comes tumbling down the stony way,
It beckons you as if it calls,
Like a fairy bright and gay.

Over the stones and rocks it gushes,
With a heavy, mighty roar,
Down the foamy falls it rushes,
With more adventures still in store.

It thunders round the river's bend,
Throwing about its wet wet spray,
And soon comes to his journey's end,
And widens out into the bay.

The Blacksmith
The blacksmith with his mighty hammer,
Beats the anvil with a clamour,
And the gusty bellows blow,
The fiery furnace into fiery glow.

With a lusty blow the shoes he bends.
He beats the iron and sparks he sends.
All the time the horses eat,
While the blacksmith shoes their feet.

Winter
Jack Frost has been again,
He makes patterns on the window pane,
Flowers, ferns and starlight things,
During the night the cold he brings.

In the morning it's a lovely sight,
Everything is tinged with white,
The grass and hedges have lost their green,
Covered with frost so ghostly seem.

Autumn

When Autumn comes the leaves all fall,
And boys and girls all shout and call,
Swirling and swivelling the leaves come down,
In yellow, orange and russet brown.

When the Autumn sun is shining bright,
And all the pretty birds take flight,
With their wings outspread and their legs tucked in,
Homeward bound as the light grows dim.

When the trees in Autumn time are bare,
And the birds sing in the sweet fresh air,
But very soon they'll be on the wing,
And won't return until next Spring.

The Coggle

Once there was a coggle,
Who tried to do a woggle,
He woggled and woggled and woggled in vain,
And so he went to Rattler Rain.

Rattler told him what to do.
'But first,' he said, 'you need a shoe.'
He woggled and woggled and woggled all day,
And then worn out, he woggled away.

When he went to bed that night,
In a dream he had a fright,
He dreamt that he was woggling on,
Woggling on till he was gone.

The River

I gurgle
Twisting and turning
I go
Babbling,
Tinkling,
Dripping over rocks
For I am a little river.
Now I am bigger
Fish swim in me
High above I see
Wellington boots.

Muddy am I
There I end in the sea
But I do not die
For high above
I am still young.

Susanna Taylor (age 6), Ecclesall Infant School, Sheffield.
Cadbury's Third book of Children's poetry (Penguin)

Man builds houses beside me
I am powerful
Suspension bridges hang over me
But I am spoiled

Advanced activities

Greetings – developments

Musical aims
To develop children's spontaneous use of their singing voices.

What you need
Voices.

What to do
It is a good idea to use some form of greetings game regularly.

- Older children are very self-conscious about it unless they have grown up with it, but it really does promote the spontaneous use of that most musical of all instruments – the voice.
- You can develop the greetings games described on pages 15 and 35 in a variety of ways as the following examples.
- A child greets the teacher first, with his or her own spontaneous tune. The teacher replies, copying the child's tune.
- The child's tune goes up, and the teacher's answer goes down.
- The child's tune is a slow one, and the teacher's is fast.

Gesture conducting

Musical aims
To develop in children the feeling experience of music.
To develop their responsiveness to leadership.
To develop imagination and fluency in leading.

What you need
Instruments.

What to do
Group the instruments according to type, or pitch or in mixed combinations of these.
- Demonstrate yourself how the instruments can be persuaded to play in whatever mood you indicate with your gestures. Use mood words such as – *smooth, calm, jerky, angry, anxious, determined, rugged, funny, heavy, floating, fussy.*
- Ask for volunteer children to replace you.
- When you split up into groups, let each group play in turn, allowing about 30 to 40 seconds for each conductor. It will not take long for every child in the class to have a turn.
- Tape record some of these, and on a future occasion play them back and ask children to draw, paint or write – expressing what the music means to them in terms of feeling and mood.

Semi-sustaining instruments

Musical aims
To help the children listen more intently to a dying sound and to realise its potential for expression.

What you need
All the ringing instruments you can find:
cymbals;
Indian bells;
triangles;
chime bars;
glockenspiel;
piano.

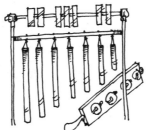

What to do
Get all the children to strike together once, and listen to the sounds fading. Decide which one lasts the longest.
● Repeat, asking children to sing (any note) at the same time. See if they can hold their vocal note as long as the longest instrument, without taking a breath.
● Try the voices without the instruments. Whose lasts the longest?
● At a signal, get the children to first strike, and then damp their instruments.
● Now give up the leadership. Split the class into groups and let as many children as possible be conductors, indicating only when to strike and when to damp. All groups can work at once. If you tape record and replay the result it will make an interesting texture of sound.
● As children become more skilful at both conducting and playing they can signal loud strikes or quiet ones.
● A further progression is to include rapid oscillations – which get as near as possible to a continuous sound. These can get louder or quieter, either gradually or suddenly.

● Develop this activity into movement, working on *creeping very slowly, suddenly freezing, making sudden short movements, gradually sinking or rising, shimmering or gliding.*

Rhythmic backing

Musical aims
To strengthen rhythmic control and independence.

What you need
Percussion instruments.
Voices.
6/8 cards from rhythm bank (pages 94–98).

What to do
Use several 6/8 cards from the rhythm bank. Divide the class into groups of about six and let each group choose one of the cards.

● Let them all practise playing their rhythms over and over again.

● Let one group start playing and after a few repetitions bring another group in. When the third group enters the first group stops and so on, so that only two groups are playing at any one moment.

It's raining, it's pouring... Diddlety, diddlety, dumpty... The old man is snoring the cat ran up the plum tree! He bumped his head on the leg of the bed...

● When things are running smoothly, chant one of the rhymes from first rhyme bank (See pages 78–81): One-ery, two-ery, tickery seven; Diddlety, diddlety dumpty or It's raining, it's pouring. Start quietly and get gradually louder. Do not expect children to join you in chanting. They will be concentrating on their own rhythms by saying and playing the rhythm words.

● Since signalling volume would complicate things too much, encourage children to play both loudly and quietly, when they like, for contrast.

● Make any variations you wish in this arrangement. For instance, a group of children could chant and move rhythmically; or two groups of children could chant two different rhymes simultaneously.

Composing a song

Musical aims
To help children to compose within a framework of known sounds.
To improve children's aural perception and imagination.

What you need
A rhyme from the second rhyme bank (See pages 82–85) or one of your own choice, or children's own writing.

What to do
Prepare children's ears for the notes to be used – any of the following three pentatonic scales:

C D E G A (*Doh Ray Me Soh Lah*)
C D F G A
D E G A B } *Soh Lah Doh Ray*

Use one of these sets of notes for improvising on instruments; signalling little tunes for voices and/or instruments; greetings or instructions.
- Choose a rhyme from second rhyme bank, and improvise tunes for it on tuned instruments (see Tuned instrument games, page 14).
- Discuss the possible rhythms you could use for the words (see Making songs, page 34) and settle for one.
- Ask all children to think of a tune and the signals for it for the first line. They should do this silently. After a short time, ask a volunteer to signal his or her tune for the others, and repeat it. All the children should then sing it, using singing names several times and then the words.
- Continue with each line of the song in the same way. The children who compose each line should remain in front signalling their line every time it is sung.

- Start again at the beginning every time a new line is added.
- When the tune is complete, get the children to learn it thoroughly and discuss speed, loudness quietness, who sings which piece, whether movement is to be added, whether there is to be an accompaniment, and so on.
- This is a model for children to work on their own, in pairs or small groups. But do make it clear that it is not the only model! It is a rather formal way of composing songs. Refer back to Making songs, page 34, for an informal approach, and use this also to balance the hard work of this section.

53

Patchwork with tunes

Musical aims
To help children become aware of form and structure in the making of tunes.

What you need
Tuned instruments – as many as possible – with all the notes, or with a pentatonic scale, as you wish.

What to do
Group the children in twos or threes, with a tuned instrument for each group.
● Get each member of each group to compose a short phrase, practise and remember it.
● Tell children that they now have two or three phrases of music that they can put together in any order they wish, repeating each one or not as they like, to make a longer piece.
● This patchwork of tunes must have a good ending, so if none of their phrases provide this, suggest that they can make another one.

Note: their idea of a good ending might not be the same as yours! Keep an open mind and at this stage be satisfied as long as they are.

Writing—1

Musical aims
To help children to make the connection between the pitch signalling system and the written notation.

What you need
Music lined paper (see page 125).
Rhythm cards (See pages 94-111).

What to do
Show children how to write blobs, either between lines, or with lines going through them. Let them write any number and check that there is a clear difference between line blobs and space blobs.

● Tell them that any blob anywhere can be *Doh*. Let one child write a blob for you on the blackboard and call it *Doh*. (Note *Doh* is in the same space as the blob).

● Continue by saying:
● 'Now if that one is *Doh*, and this one is *Ray* (write), can you write the *Me* blob for me?

• Most children will now catch on, but a few may need help in differentiating between line and space blobs.

• Encourage the children to sing as they write and go round the class singing everyone's tune to and with them.

• Ask them to decide how many times they would like their tune sung and let them write it out that number of times with a bar line between each, and a double bar line for the end.

• Let the children choose a rhythm each and ask them to copy it exactly over their music lines, for example:

• Note that we have only been tackling one concept in this activity: the relationship between the sound of neighbour notes and the writing of neighbour notes. If this is properly absorbed, everything else will follow.

• Now ask them to write the same blobs on the *Doh*, *Ray* or *Me* lines or space and attach the stems to them.

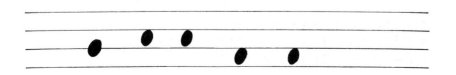

A different set of notes

Musical aims
Aural preparation for further understanding of pitch relationships.

What you need
Tuned instruments using the notes, C D E F G A (*Doh Ray Me Fah Soh Lah*).

What to do
Explain that you are going to use these six notes because there are many well-known tunes that use them.
- Let the children try to work out for themselves the tune of *Twinkle Twinkle Little Star*. Give them the first notes and a few clues if they are getting lost, but do not help unnecessarily.

- Go through the usual preparation games – signalling, improvising on instruments, greeting instructions, copying games and so on.
- Let them work out any of these tunes by ear.
- Let them use the six notes for composing tunes to any rhymes or poems.

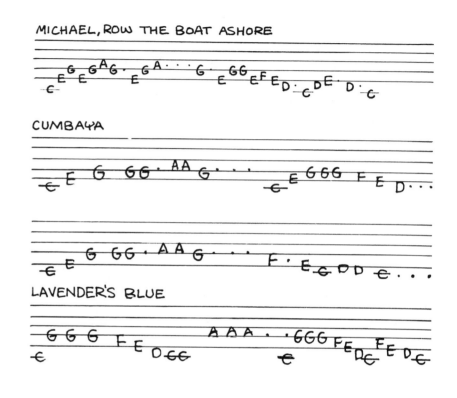

- In practising vocal reading, introduce *Fah* slowly at first in conjunction with *Doh Ray* and *Me* and later in conjunction with *Soh* and *Lah*.
- Finally experiment in front of the children with the six notes in key F (ie with F as *Doh*) and another six in key G (ie with G as *Doh*). In the case of F, you will find that B sounds wrong. Replace it with B♭ (flat).
- These six notes may now gradually be extended into writing, as in Patchwork with tunes on page 54.

Fun with scales

Musical aims
To accustom children to the sound of scales of different types.
To help them to develop rhythmic imagination.

What you need
Xylophone.

What to do
So far only the five-note pentatonic scales have been used as follows:

1. Doh ray me soh lah
2. Soh lah doh ray me
3. Soh lah doh ray me

- Now fill in the gaps to make the complete seven-note scales. Try these with the children. Treating C as *Doh*, sing up the whole scale – *Doh Ray Me Fah Soh Lah Te Doh* and down again (backwards).
- Now let a child play it on a xylophone.
- The game is to sing or play this scale up and down, using all kinds of different rhythms, slow and quick, in all combinations. Now try the same procedure with G as *Doh*. Let the children feel the wrongness of the note *Te* (F) and replace it with F# (sharp).
- Repeat this procedure with F as *Doh* and replace the B with B♭ (flat).
- Combine work with rhythm cards and percussion instruments to one of these scales.

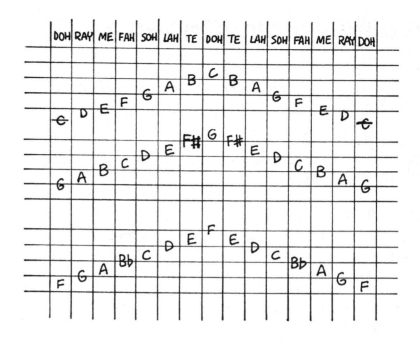

Note: if several tuned instruments are being used in one room, it is easier on everyone's ears if they use the notes of only one scale.

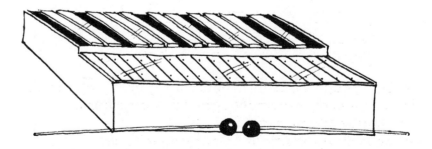

57

Notes for *The Drunken Sailor* and others

Musical aims

Aural preparation for further understanding of pitch relationships.

What you need

Tuned instruments using the notes C D E F G and A, with C as *Doh*.

What to do

Remove low C from the instrument. Do some aural preparation games (see the previous activity) using D E F G A B C.

● Help the children to work out *What Shall We Do With the Drunken Sailor?* by ear. As usual, be content if some children only manage one phrase and let them have the satisfaction of playing it in the right place.

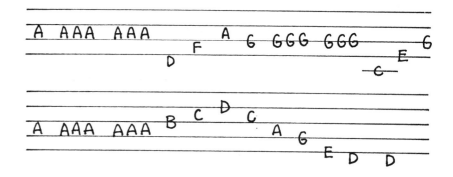

● As you improvise on these notes, you will probably get the feeling that D or *Ray* is the home note or *key note* as it is usually called. (It is the removal of C that gives this effect. Once you have the feeling that D is your key note rather than C, you may return C to the instrument). Call this set of notes the *Ray mode*.

- Encourage children to use the *Ray* mode for composing instrumental tunes. Talk to them about the feeling that this particular mode has for them and ask them to compose character pieces, expressing the same feeling that they experienced. (Do not expect these feelings to be the same for everyone).
- The basic set of notes, with slight variation, is used for *The Tailor and the Mouse, Greensleeves* and other folk tunes.
- It is important now to encourage children at all times to come up with their own set of notes, modes or scales for use in composing. There are considerably cultural differences in this respect and children might find something nearer to their own cultural roots if they are allowed to explore freely.
- For this purpose chromatic instruments are essential, and children should be encouraged to use both black and white notes. It should be made absolutely clear that in musical terms black and white notes are indistinguishable.
- To prove it, ask children to shut their eyes. Ask a child to come and play notes at random and ask the others if they are white or black.

Atmospherics in sound

Musical aims
To help children gain a finer control of their instruments and a sensitivity to sound.

What you need
Any instruments, voices. Tape recorder.

What to do
Start with the whole class. Describe a large, slow circle, like a clock, with your hand. Make this action last at least twenty seconds, moving in an anti-clockwise direction for you, so that it is clockwise for the children. Ask the children to play only one, quiet sound each during your circle, doing so at any point they like.

- Now make more circles – as many as you think appropriate, and tell the children:

- 'In the first circle, make one quiet sound on your instrument. In the second circle, imitate this sound with your voice. In the third circle make a different quiet sound with your instrument. In the fourth circle, imitate it with your voice.' And so on.

- Be prepared for laughter when the voices are used but persevere till it dies down. Tape record some of the sounds and discuss them.

- Once the circle technique has been established, give some different instructions, such as:

- 'One loud note and two quiet ones per circle', or 'One vocal note to any vowel you like or a *mm* or *ng* lasting only as long as you have breath'; or 'One very quiet shake – long or short'.

- And, of course, as soon as possible, get children to lead. You could continue doing the circle (children find it hard to keep it slow enough) and they could give the instructions.

- If you do a series of circles with more happening in each circle; you will get a build-up. You can try the same idea the other way round – starting with a lot happening, and progressively asking for less and less.

Variation
Instead of single sounds ask children to play the rhythms of such things as: their own names, the first line of a nursery rhyme or any other words. Or they could play Character rhythms (see page 41).

- However, it is a good idea to keep to short phrases or the sound becomes overloaded.

Action replay

Musical aims
To develop sensitivity to sound and its symbolic meaning. To develop memory for non-rhythmic music.

What you need
Any instruments.

What to do
Choose a leader, who should have a magic stick (see page 8). As each person is pointed at he or she must play for no more than five seconds, starting very quietly, gradually increasing and fading again, all within the five seconds. The conductor may choose how often the different players are pointed at.

could be a little bit of the kind of sport seen on television football, tennis etc, or it could be some very short scene occurring in the news or a soap opera or other drama. The condition is that once it has been played, it must be re-played. Let children make and use graphic notation cards (See page 87).

● Next, conductors say how players are to play when they are pointed at.

● This game may be done also in smaller groups but in this case, have periods in which only one group at a time is working, in order to encourage good listening. If conductors need suggestions for their instructions the following might be helpful: Start with a bang and fade rapidly; try three short, quiet sounds and one loud one; use one phrase and one echo.

● Now ask for an action replay. A conductor points the magic stick at the players in a certain order, having told them what they are to play. The whole exercise is repeated once or twice. Each group then plays its piece at least twice to the others.

● Another form of this game could involve each group discussing a short scene that they could depict in sound. It

Sequence and variation

Musical aims
To help children become aware of two very common features of traditional music.

What you need
Tuned instruments using a complete scale.

What to do for 'Sequence'
Ask a child to compose a very short phrase on an instrument. Everyone should sing it, and as many as possible play it.
● Ask the same child or another to play the same tune again, but starting on a next door note – either one higher or one lower. Continue repeating this tune, always starting it one step away from the previous version.

Note: children usually invent this way of composing at some time and it is important that the teacher should recognise it and draw the child's attention to it when it appears.
● Examples occur very frequently in real music. The song 'I Believe' starts with a long phrase, 'I believe for ev'ry drop of rain that falls, a flower grows'. The music of which is repeated, two notes higher, for 'I believe that somewhere in the darkest night a candle glows', and again, two notes higher, for 'I believe for ev'ry one who goes astray someone will come' and one note higher, 'to show the way'.
● The first phrase of 'Side by Side', 'Oh, we ain't got a barrel of money' is repeated, two notes higher, for 'May be we're ragged and funny.'
● And, in the middle eight, the first phrase, 'Thro' all kinds of weather, What if they sky should fall?' is repeated, one note lower, for 'Just as long as we're together, It doesn't matter at all'.
● In 'Do-Re-Me', the music for the first phrase 'Doe, a deer, a female deer' is repeated, two notes higher for 'Me, a name I call myself'. The music for the second phrase, 'Ray, a drop of golden sun' is repeated, two notes higher, for 'Far, a long long way to run'. And then three phrases follow, in sequence (one rising step each time):
'Sew, a needle pulling thread'
'La, a note to follow sew'
'Tea, a drink with jam and bread'
before the conclusion, 'that will bring us back to Doe'.

What to do for 'Variation'

Play a very simple tune, such as the one below.

- Ask everyone to sing it. Get three or four children to play it again and again.
- Everyone else sings along, making all kinds of *rhythm* variations. As children get bolder, invite them to vary the tune during the G notes but making sure they land on A on time.
- Vocalists have always improvised variations in their songs. If you taught the children a straight version of *Side by side* and then played them a recorded version by any well-known artist they would immediately understand what a variation is.

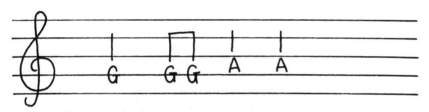

- A classical example of simple variations is furnished by Bizet in a version of the *Farandole* *(these variations are readily appreciated by six- and seven-year olds, the changing moods of each are ideal for movement).

* 'Prelude' from L'Arlesienne Suite No. 2.

Two tunes at once

Musical aims
To make children aware of the musical possibilities of combining tunes.

What you need
Any tuned instruments, or voices, using all the notes of a scale. Tape recorder.

What to do
Suggest to children that any tune, either one of their own or an existing one, could have a second tune or friend to go along with it.

• Like a real person, this friend could be either very similar to the tune or very different from it.

• Ask a child to make up and repeat a very short tune on an instrument. Everybody sings it, and as many as possible play it.

• Ask another child to play the same tune but starting on a different note. Try both tunes together in parallel, and ask for everyone's comments.

• Repeat this, starting the second parallel tune on yet another note. See if there is a consensus on which of the parallel tunes sounds best in conjunction with the original tune. Try starting on other notes.

• Now try a similar process trying to combine very different tunes. Ask a child to compose, say, a very slow tune. Everyone should repeat it as before. Observe which notes have been used and ask a second child to improvise a second tune, firstly using a different set of notes from the first child, and then moving quickly and in a contrasting way to the slow tune.

• Let many children improvise second tunes. Tape record them and later play them back.

• Play the children examples of real music. Parallel tunes are so common that almost any popular song would provide an example or any version of *Silent Night*.

• Contrasting tunes are exemplified in a very clear way in Bizet's *Farandole* (from *L'Arlesienne* suite *No 1*). Children could well be asked to move to this, as soldiers marching, contrasting with children running, or whatever suggestions they might offer.

Writing—2

Musical aims
To help and further children's understanding of notation especially as applied to instruments.

What you need
Any tuned instruments.

What to do
Explain that in music the singing names of notes (*Doh* etc) can be anywhere — high, low or medium. (Sing *Doh Ray Me* at several different pitches).
- But the instrument names (A B C D E F G) are fixed, are printed on the instruments and are the same the world over.
- Show them the sign 𝄞 at the beginning of a piece of music and explain that it is an old fashioned capital G and that it shows where G has to be on the music lines.

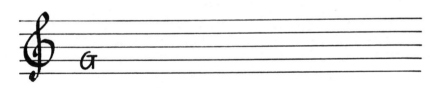

- Let children look at the note G on their instruments and ask them the name of the note that is one higher. Write it like this:

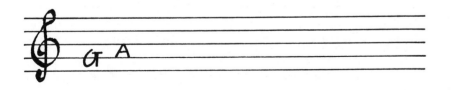

- Ask them to write in the next note B, and the remaining notes:

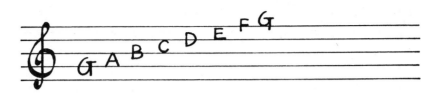

- And then go downwards.

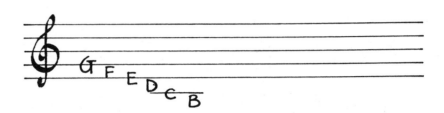

- Explain how, if they run off the bottom line they have to have a little extra line (or two sometimes) as in C and B.
- Finally explain that instead of writing the letters musicians use blobs.

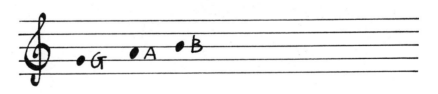

- Get them to write blobs anywhere they like with the letter names beside.
- Some children may be lost at this stage. In case they are, concentrate on just a few notes and help them by writing a few letter names on the music lines, and then a few blobs as follows:

- Show the children how to read from left to right, along the lines, from the letter to the blob.
- Since children cannot possibly be expected to remember all the notes, teachers should only use a few at a time, for practice. At this stage the important thing is to show children how to work it out.

Chords – experiments

Musical aims
To stimulate children to listen to and become more aware of combinations of notes and their musical possibilities.

What you need
Tuned instruments of any sort, using the complete scale of C D E F G A B C etc. Tape recorder.

What to do
Divide the class into groups of three if possible, or larger groups if necessary.
- Let them work as far away from each other as possible. Ask each group to find a set of notes that sound good together.
- When all the groups have done this (it should take very little time) appoint a conductor with a magic stick. Each group plays its chord as the conductor directs (*loud, quiet, once, many times* etc). Give several children turns at conducting, and discuss with them which chords they like, what the notes are, which follows which best, what feelings or pictures they conjure up. A tape recorder is very useful here.
- Try a few examples of two chords at once. If some sound good and some bad, try to work out why.
- In this activity you are no more or less knowledgeable than the children. It is all a matter of opinion – as indeed are many other of the activities.
- In the next activity traditional practice will be described.

Chords – traditional practice

Musical aims
To help children to become more aware of chords they already 'Know' by sound.

What you need
Tuned instruments.

What to do
Children hear chorded accompaniment from an early age, whether on radio or on the school piano. However, they do not usually appear to be very interested in harmony (ie the use of combinations of sounds) until they are nine at the youngest.

● The principles governing the use of harmony in western music are fairly simple. In any music of a traditional nature, there are several things happening at once. But one element – the tune – stands out from the rest.

● It stands out because it is either higher or louder (or both) than the rest and because it is more interesting. Thus, in pop music, the main interest is on the song and the rest is called the *backing*.

● The song is often more interesting than the backing because it has more movement. In western music certain features almost always appear.

● The movement of a tune tends to be quicker than the backing and stands out from it. It is quite recognisable even without the backing.

● The backing or *accompaniment* (to give it its highbrow name) is specifically required to be less interesting and to move about more slowly, or at least less obtrusively, than the tune. Consequently if detached from its tune it is

WAA WAAA WAAAHH

probably unrecognisable except by an expert.

● How does a composer make the tune and the backing fit together? As a general principle, he or she uses notes in the backing that are prominent (ie often used) in the tune.

● With children, the best approach to laying the foundation for their possible future work with chords, is an aural one.

● If you are a pianist or guitarist, play a single major chord on the piano or guitar in a neutral way, and ask the children to sing with you any tunes that fit. These can be high and low, fast and slow, scales or jumps, smooth or jerky – depending on what feels right. If you are not a **player get a colleague to do it for you.**

● If you have enough instruments, let groups of children improvise as follows:

● For the C chord use notes C (D) E (F), for the A minor chord, use notes A (B) C (D). The notes actually being played in the chord are the unbracketed ones. The bracketed ones might well feature as passing notes in the tunes that children improvise.

● Do not have more than three children improvising at any one time, for it is most important that they hear what they are doing.

Variation

Let the children use notes C (D) E G (A) or A (B) C (D) E (G). The next stage is to let them hear and improvise vocally to two changing chords. Firstly, play the *Doh* chord and *Soh* chord. Secondly (when *Ray* is the key note) play the *Ray* chord and the *Doh* chord.

● Finally, using the notes they used before, let them improvise instrumentally over the changing chords.

● All this improvisation work should precede and continue alongside any reading work they may be doing.

Chords – reading the symbols

Musical aims
To further children's understanding of chords as used in songbooks and to improve their facility in using them.

What you need
Tuned instruments. Copies of page 122.

What to do
Give the children copies of O *Sinner man* (see page 122). Tell them to look at the chord symbols and to play the note of the appropriate letter, as they see it. In this case they should play:

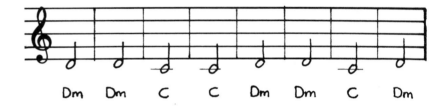

● Then tell them that the chord note can also be joined by another note – the next but one upwards. In this case it is F. They should now play:

- This chord scheme will also serve to accompany *What Shall We Do with the Drunken Sailor?*
- The *m* of Dm means D minor, but at present it would be too complicated and unnecessary to explain this term.
- Chords usually contain three or four notes, but at this stage two is plenty, and the sound is adequate. At a later date let them supply the chords for *Colon Man* (see page 124). (Note that F# is required for this tune and the chords as well.)

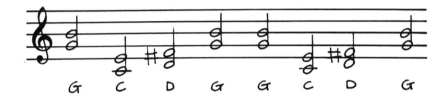

G   C   D   G   G   C   D   G

- On the same basis children can supply chords for all the songs in the Reproducible material.

Make a round—2

Musical aims
To reinforce harmonic feeling by singing in round.
To harness children's inventiveness to the round form.

What you need
Voices.

What to do
Sing a well-known round with the children. *Frère Jacques* is suitable – or you could use *Three small cars* or *Kukaburra*, see pages 121 and 123.

To analyse the round, ask the following questions.
The words: do they rhyme?
The music: is any section of a round like any other section? The sections of *Frère Jacques* are:

1 – *Frère Jacques, Frère Jacques.*
2 – *Dormez-vous, dormez-vous?*
3 – *Sonnez la mattine, sonnez la mattine.*
4 – *Ding-dong-dong, ding-dong-dong.*

- Are all the sections sung together?
- Do some bits go faster or slower than others?
- Are there more words in some sections than in others?
- Children should conclude that words do not have to rhyme, and that no section of a round has a tune the same as another section. They should also realise that all the sections are sung together, as all voices join in. These sections combine well, some bits can go much faster than others and some sections have many more words than others.
- Remembering these points, find or make some words for a round. This example uses three proverbs:

A watched pot never boils
You can take a horse to water, but you can't make it drink
East, west, home's best

- Clearly the longest proverb will have to go quickly in order to fit with the shortest, which will have to go slowly. (Accent marks are used to indicate strong beats).
You can tàke a horse to wàter but you càn't make it drìnk.

Let the children work in pairs to try to fit the second and third proverbs together in speech.

Later they can work in threes to get all three to fit.

Choose one of the successful trios, and teach their version to the whole class (still using speech). When it is learned, let a group of children work out a simple two-chord progression to accompany it. Let them repeat this progression over and over and invite children now to sing instead of speaking, one line at a time.

Do the same with the other two proverbs. If each tune fits with the chords, they will all fit together.

Making a music-story or drama

Musical aims
To reinforce previous work by using skills they have already learned to compose music for a story or drama.

What you need
Stories made up by children or the ones suggested.
Instruments of all types.
Voices, and a tape recorder.

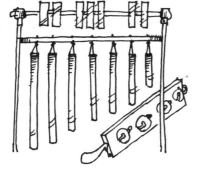

What to do
Teachers will have many ideas from stories they have used regularly. The only problem is to find stories that lend themselves to musical treatment. Traditional stories can be very good sources here. Grimm's versions of folk tales are often very suitable, because of their distinct differentiation of character. Sybil Marshall's *Everyman's Book of English Folk Tales* (Dent) includes some excellent stories of which two are worth special mention: *The Fairy Fetch* and the *Weardale Fairies*. These appeal to children's love of the supernatural. Some parts of Greek legends are also good, so are Aesop's fables.

In summary, stories that have a strong element of fantasy are best for musical and dramatic treatment. The two that follow are good examples.

No suggestions are made for the music, since it is hoped that children who have used the activities explored in this book will have plenty of ideas for both composition and performance. But there are suggestions as to where the music should fall, and what it should illustrate.

How snakes and other reptiles came into the world—A folk tale from Ghana

Once upon a time there lived a lively little boy called Rickey (*music*). One day he was sent to wash some plates by the side of the river. Whilst he was washing them, one was carried away by the water. He tried to recover it but failed. He was very sad and, as he made his way home, he started crying (*music*).

71

All of a sudden, he saw an old woman walking slowly along the road (*music*). She called Rickey and asked him why he was crying. He told the old woman what had happened to him, and she told him:

'Never mind, I will help you to get everything you want. What is your wish my little boy?'

'I wish we had a beautiful house with everything we need already in it,' said Rickey.

'If you obey and keep to my instructions your wish will be granted,' said, the old woman. 'Walk straight on until you come to the crossroads. Turn right, then follow the road. It will lead you to a house with a blue door. Go into the house. On the table in the sitting room you will find two baskets of eggs. The eggs in one basket will be saying "Take me. Take me" and those in the other basket will say "Don't take me, don't take me." Take just one egg from the "Don't take me" basket.'

Rickey said 'thank you' to the old woman, and left. (*Rickey's music*).

When he got to the house, he listened carefully to what the eggs were saying (*two kinds of egg music*). He took an egg from "Don't take me" basket and went home.

When he got there, he made his wish and smashed the egg (*music*). At once, a beautiful house appeared with everything the family needed in it. Rickey was very happy.

A few weeks later the woman next door sent her own naughty little boy to go to wash some plates by the side of the river. His name was Jim (*Jim's music*). While he was there, a plate was carried away but he did not make any effort to recover it. On his way home he thought to himself:

'What am I going to tell mama about the missing plate?'

The old woman appeared again (*music*). Once again, asked the boy to make a wish, and he also asked for a beautiful house. The old woman gave him exactly the same instructions as she had given Rickey.

But Jim did not say 'thank you'. Instead he ran all the way until he got to the house (*Jim's music*). As soon as he opened the door, he heard the eggs in one basket saying 'Take me, take me' (*music*) and the eggs in the other basket saying 'Don't take me. Don't take me' (*music*).

Jim stood there for a while and then said to himself:

'The old woman must have made a mistake, I shall take one from the "take me" basket.'

72

So that is what he did. He grabbed an egg, and rushed home. Like Rickey, he made a wish and smashed the egg (*music*). But instead of a beautiful house, all sorts of snakes, lizards and other reptiles appeared (*music*). Jim and his mother had to run away from their home, and that is how snakes and other reptiles came into the world.

You will also need to compose two songs:

1   Old woman's instructions
2   Final song

You will need seven pieces of music:

1   Music for Rickey when he is happy and when he is sad
2   Music for the old woman
3   Music for the 'take me' eggs
4   Music for the 'don't take me eggs'
5   Music for the egg breaking and the house appearing
6   Music for Jim
7   Music for snakes, lizards and reptiles

The Princess of Tomboso

An old man lay dying (*music*).

Round his bed stood his three sons. They were waiting to hear what he was trying to say to them. At last they caught his words:

'Presents – for all of you – in the big urn.'

With those words on his lips, he died.

The three sons at once went to see what was in the urn.

First they drew out a purse (*music*), then a belt (*music*) and finally a bugle (*music*).

On the purse was written:

'Empty me as often as you like.'

They emptied all the money out, shut the purse, and there it was, full again.

On the belt was written:

'Put me on, and I will take you wherever you want to go, without delay.'

On the bugle was written:

'If you want an army, blow three calls on me.'

They decided not to try out the belt and the bugle just yet.

Now the youngest son was called Joe (*music*). He immediately made up his mind that he wanted to go and marry the beautiful Princess of Tomboso, who lived in the castle a few miles off (*music*). So, without thinking of the consequences, he put on the belt and said: 'Take me to the Princess of Tomboso's private room ' (*music*).

He was there in a flash. The Princess was doing her hair at the time, and you can imagine her surprise at seeing an intruder in her room.

'How on earth did you get here?' she asked. Joe told her all about the magic belt.

Now the Princess was clever (*music*). She easily persuaded Joe to lend her the belt.

'To my father's office!' she cried, and was gone (*music*).

Presently some soldiers came, gave Joe a good beating, and threw him out of the castle gates (*music*).

Joe limped home, (*music*) and brought the bad news to his brothers.

When he'd recovered, he thought:

'If I take the purse, (*music*) I'll be able to buy back the belt.

With difficulty, he persuaded his brothers to let him have the purse. This time he had to walk to the castle (*music*).

The Princess was in her room (*music*) when he knocked. She was very surprised to see Joe again, but pretended to welcome him.

When he showed her the purse, and offered her a thousand pounds for the return of his belt, she chided him:

'I don't believe it's magic at all!'

'Well', said simple Joe, 'Why don't you try it?' (*music*).

Of course, that was the last he saw of the purse!

It was a sadder and sorrier Joe who returned home that night! (*music*).

There was only one thing to do – that was to take the bugle (*music*). His brothers were against it, but he managed to persuade them.

This time he met the Princess as she was driving out of the castle gates (*music*).

He threatened at once to blow the bugle; but the Princess smiled so sweetly at him, and seemed so friendly, that he didn't. But too late – in a second she grabbed the bugle from him and blew it (music) there before him was an army of soldiers. (*March and halt*). Before he could turn round he was being beaten and trampled upon by hundreds of soldiers. They left him half dead (*music*).

When Joe came to he found himself in an orchard, though how he got there he never knew. He was bruised and aching. However, he was glad to see some apples on a tree, and picked one.

No sooner did he start to eat than he felt something happening to his nose. It was growing bigger and bigger and bigger and bigger – until it was so heavy he couldn't hold his head up. He didn't know what to do, but he was still hungry so he reached out and pulled a plum off the nearest tree. Suddenly he felt something else happening to his nose. It was getting smaller and smaller and smaller and smaller – until it was back to normal.

Joe sat and thought (*music*). Suddenly he had an idea. He picked some apples, the nicest he could find and took them to the castle, as a present for the princess. He handed them to a servant at the gates, and soon the Princess was trying one. Sure enough her nose began to grow bigger and bigger and bigger and bigger, whilst she sat and screamed.

All the finest doctors in the land were sent for, but none of them could help. Finally, Joe disguised himself as a doctor and offered to help. But, he said, before he could help her, he must ask if she had anything on her conscience, any tricks she had played, anything she had taken from anyone?

'Well – yes –,' she said, giving him the belt (*music*).

grandchildren the story of their old father (*music*) of Joe (*music*) and the Princess (*music*) and of the three gifts – the purse (*music*) the belt (*music*) and the bugle (*music*).

You will need music for:
1. The old man on his death bed
2. The purse
3. The belt } This should include singing their words
4. The bugle
5. Joe
6. The princess
7. The soldiers
8. Various magic transformations.

You will also need songs for:
1. Joe (several opportunities)
2. The princess (several opportunities)
3. The brothers

'Anything else?' asked Joe.
'Well – er – well – er, just this,' said she, giving him the purse (*music*).
'Anything else?' Joe asked again.
'Well, er – not really – well – only this,' said she, handing over the bugle (*music*).
'Ah!' said Joe. 'Now here is your medicine.'

   As the Princess ate the plum, her nose grew smaller and smaller and smaller and smaller until it was the right size. By this time, Joe had put on the belt and cast off his disguise.

   'Away home!' he shouted, and disappeared with his precious treasures.

   Joe and his brothers lived in comfort for the rest of their lives, but none of them thought of marrying the princess. They married girls from their village and were quite content. Years later they often told their children and their

Rhyme bank 1

1
One, two, buckle my shoe,
Three, four, knock at the door,
Five, six, pick up sticks,
Seven, eight, lay them straight,
Nine, ten, a big fat hen.

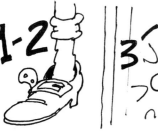

2
Bell-horses, bell-horses,
What time of day?
One o'clock, two o'clock,
Off and away.

3
Leg over, leg over,
The dog went to Dover
He came to a stile,
Then he jumped over.

4
Rub-a dub dub
Three men in a tub
And who do you think they be?
The butcher, the baker, the candlestick maker,
Turn them out, knaves all three!

5
One-ery, two-ery, tickery, seven
Aliby, crackaby, ten and eleven
Pin pan, musky dan,
Twiddleum, twoddleum, twenty one.

6

Deedle deedle dumpling, my son John
Went to bed with his trousers on.
One sock off and one sock on,
Deedle deedle dumpling, my son John.

7

There was a monkey climbed a tree
When he fell down, then down fell he.

8

Diddlety, diddlety, dumpty
The cat ran up the plum tree,
Half a crown to fetch her down
Diddlety, diddlety, dumpty.

9

One to make ready
And two to prepare,
Good luck to the rider
Away goes the mare.

10

It's raining, it's pouring
The old man's snoring.
He bumped his head on the back of the bed,
And couldn't get up in the morning.

11

Chick, chick chatterman, how much are your geese?
Chick, chick, chatterman, twenty pence a-piece.
Chick, chick, chatterman, that's too dear.
Chick, chick, chatterman, chase you out of here.

12

Tinker, tailor, soldier, sailor
Rich man, poor man, beggarman, thief.

13

Peter, Peter pumpkin eater,
Had a wife and couldn't keep her.
Put her in a pumpkin shell,
There he kept her very well.

14

Vizzery, vazzery, vozzery, vem
Tizzery, tazzery, tozzery, tem
Hiram, jiram, cockrem, spirem
Poplar, rollin, gem.

15

One, two, three, four, Mary's at the cottage door
Five, six, seven, eight, eating cherries off a plate.

16

Intery, mintery, cutery corn
Apple seed and apple thorn,
Wire, brier, limber, lock
Three geese in a flock,
One flew east and one flew west,
And one flew over the cuckoo's nest.

Rhyme bank 2

The Rooks

The Rooks are alive
On the tops of the trees;
they look like a hive
Of busy black bees;
They all squawk together,
And loud is their squawking —
It must be the weather
That sets them a-talking.

The Leaves

The leaves had a wonderful frolic,
They danced to the winds's loud song,
They whirled, and they floated, and scampered,
They circled and flew along.

The moon saw the little leaves dancing,
Each looked like a small brown bird.
The man in the moon smiled and listened,
And this is the song he heard:

The North Wind is calling, is calling,
And we must whirl round and round.
And then when our dancing is ended
We'll make a warm quilt for the ground.

(from A Book of a Thousand Poems)

Anon

First Spring Morning

Open the window!
A chaffinch sings
And the sun on the lawn
Its rich gold flings;
Purple the buds
Upon the trees,
And oh, how lovely
The sap-sweet breeze!

Open the window!
The daisies' eyes
Are wide-awake
As if in surprise,
And the humble-bee's sailing
Among the flowers,
Tasting the Spring's
First Joyous hours!

Malcolm Hemphrey

83

North and South Winds

The North Wind swooped through the branches bare,
And he roared and howled all day.
He drove the sheep from the mountain-side,
And the children in from play.
He sent the snowflakes scurrying down
From a wild and bitter sky.
'Oh, I am king of the earth!' he cried,
'There's none so strong as I!'

The South Wind stirred and gently sighed,
And a tender breath she blew,
And the clouds grew pale and melted away,
And a sunbeam filtered through.
She whispered, 'Wake!' to the sleeping trees,
And she called to each dreaming flower,
And the whole land blossomed and smiled again,
Set free from the North Wind's power.

Marguerite Turnbull

Time to Get Up!

It's time to get up,' crowed the rooster,
'It's time to get up,' crowed he.

But how can he tell?
There isn't a bell!

He can't tell the time,
There isn't a chime!

He can't hear 'tick-tock,'
There isn't a clock.

So *how* does he know?
That cock who WILL crow!

O, how can it be?
For he can't tell the time, –
Like ME!

Hilda I Rostron

Catching the Train

Tick! Tock!
Warns the clock,
Hurry!
Don't be late,
Hurry!
Time is speeding on,
Remember –
Trains *won't wait*!

Elizabeth Gould

Clock-Talk

'Tick-Tick, tick-tick,
It's nice to be quiet,'
Says the little green clock on the shelf.
'Tick, tock,'
Says the big chiming-clock,
'I'd rather go slower myself.'

'Tock! tock!
Says the grandfather clock,
'this is the pace I like best:
It may seem too slow,
Yet it can't be, you know,
For I always keep time with the rest.'

Godfrey Young

Train Wheels

Clickety clack,
Clickety clack,
We are the wheels that go
Clickety clack.
Now in a tunnel,
Then up a hill,
Straight through a station,
Whizzing round still;
Faster than ever,
Past a hay-stack,
Faster and faster —
Clickety clack.

W O'Neill

Blackberry Days

The Sun wakes late
In a golden haze;
Pleasant and calm
Are Blackberry Days.

Blackberry weather
Is warm and mellow;
But elm-tree tops
Are splashed with yellow.

Dew lies long
On the orchard grass;
Low in the sky
The swallows pass.

Gossamers hang
Where the children ramble
Picking the fruit
From the wayside bramble

Berta Lawrence

All poems are extracted from *Child Education*

85

Reproducible material

Graphic notation

Sound is very difficult to describe visually. Traditional notation has to be learned, often painfully, and often at the expense of a love for music. So it is very important in the early stages to make this sight – sound connection as obvious as possible. Graphic notation tries to do this.

Firstly, size of writing reflects volume of the music. Big signs reflect big sounds, small signs reflect small sounds. So, in the rhymes, the big writing will be spoken loudly, and the little writing, quietly.

The other signs (a) ⩘⩘⩘ (b) ▌ (c) ◀▬ are my interpretations of (a) shakes, (b) bangs (c) a ringing sound that dies away.

Children can well devise their own signs.

1 2 3 4	Mary's at the Cottage door
5 6 7 8	Eating cherries off a plate
1 2 3 4	Mary's at the cottage door
5 6 7 8	Eating cherries off a plate

For any instruments

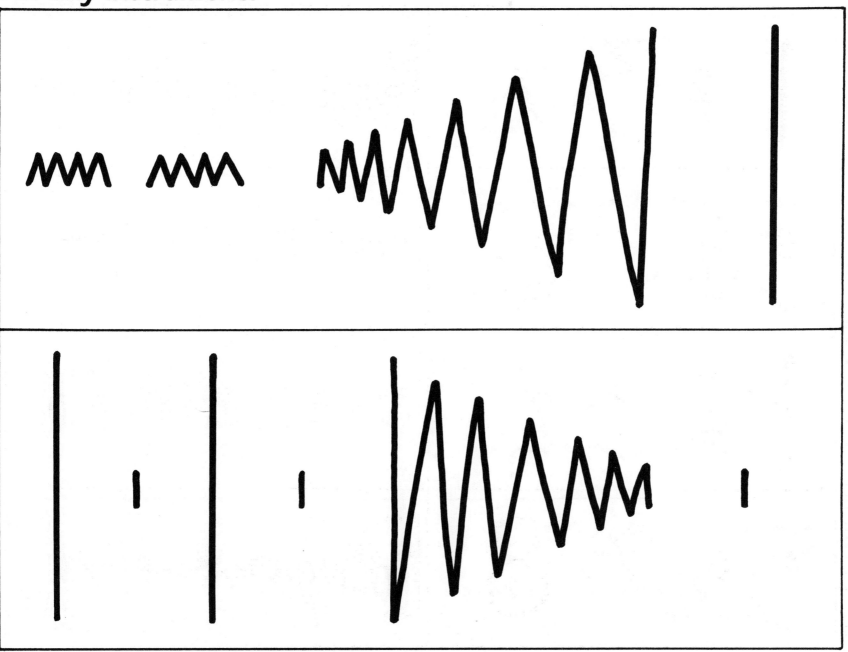

1 2 3 4	Mary's at the cott-age door
5 6 7 8	Eat-ing cher-ries off a plate
1 2 3 4	Mary's at the cot-tage door
5 6 7 8	Eating cherries off a plate

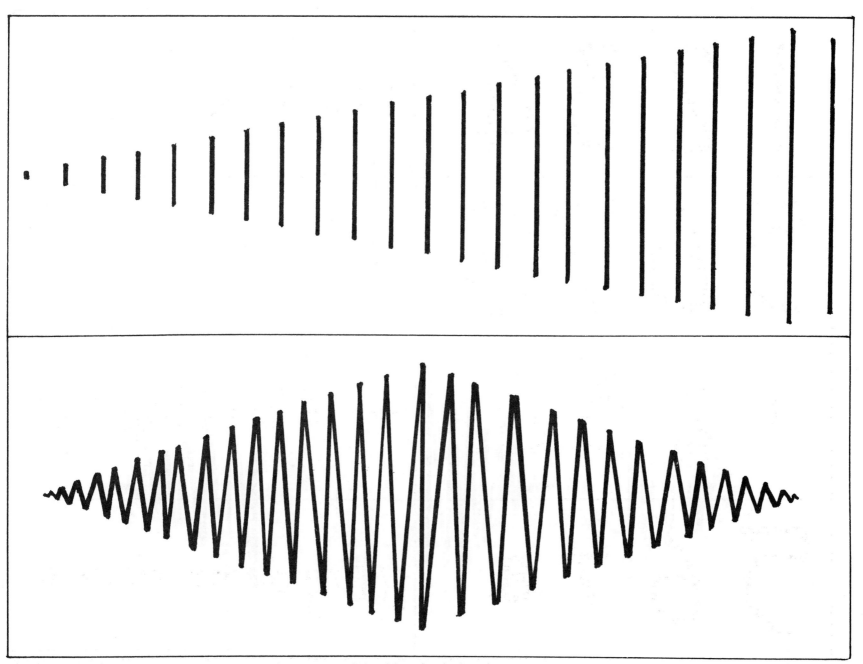

This page may be photocopied for use in the classroom and should not be declared in any return in respect of any photocopying licence.

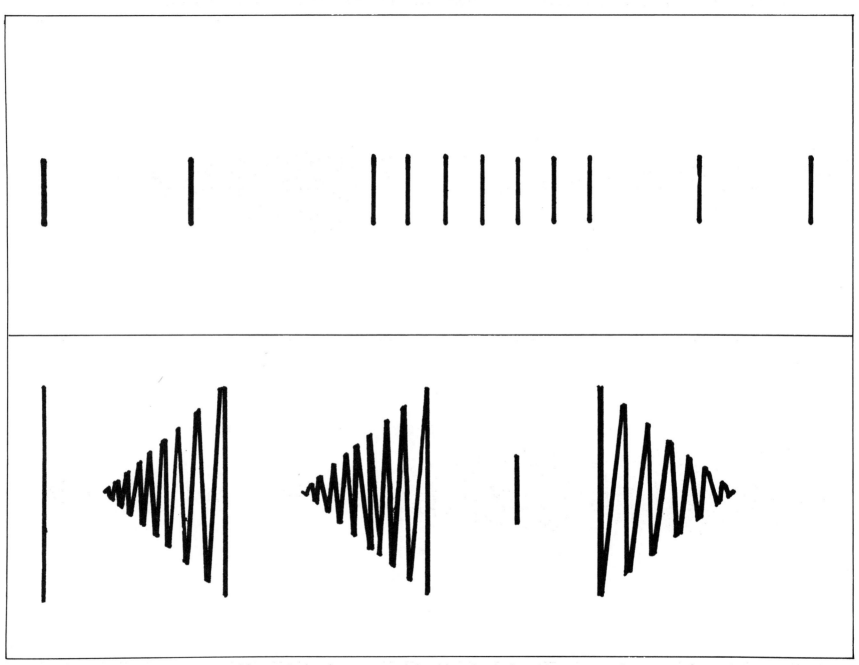

For ringing instruments – cymbals, triangles, bells etc

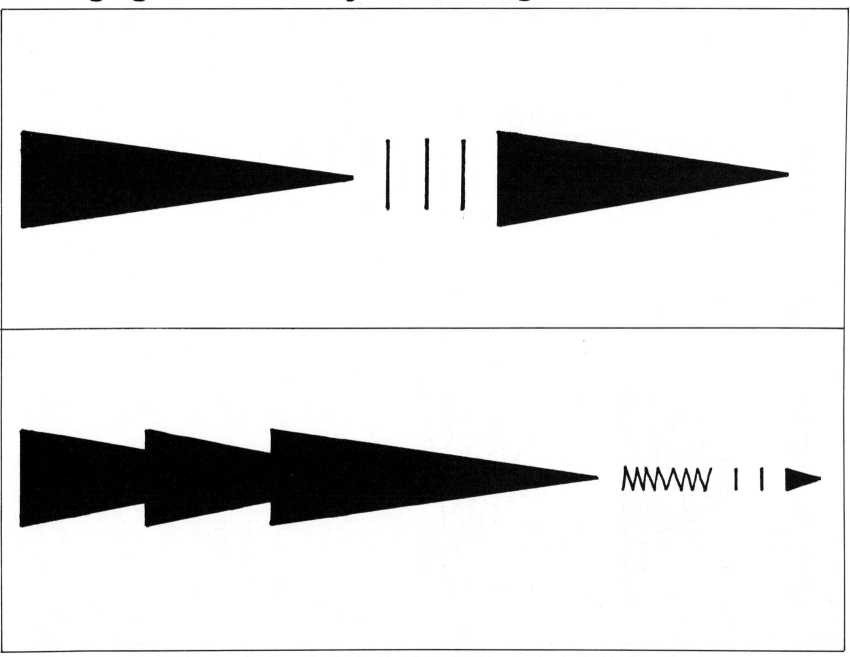

Rhythms 1
6/8 (six eight) time

The best way to acquire good rhythmic sense is by
listening and imitating. If you watch the appropriate signs
as you listen, you will almost certainly make the aural-
visual connection as well. Children do this without
explanation.

The mathematical proportions are:

if ♪ represents one unit of time

♩ represents two units

♩. represents three units

𝅗𝅥 represents four units

So ♪ goes three times as fast as ♩.

or twice as fast as ♩

or four times as fast as 𝅗𝅥

♩ goes twice as fast as 𝅗𝅥

Only one type of rest (silence) is used. 𝄽 = ♩
Children should watch and point at the cards as they
are chanted – never more than one card at a time to start
with.

As they gain experience they can play from them,
improvise melodies from them, both vocally and
instrumentally; and when they use more than one,
arrange them in various orders.

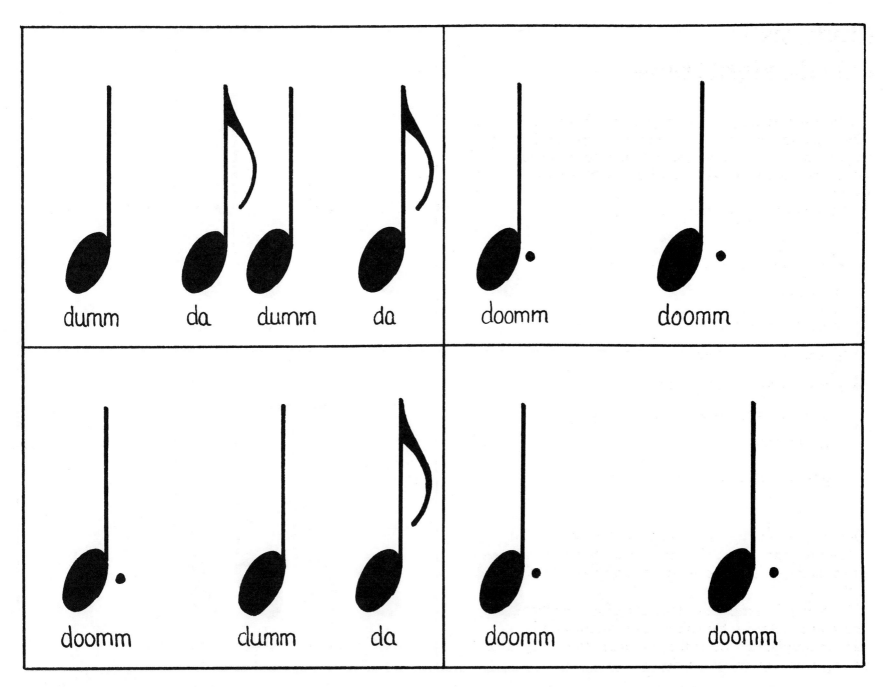

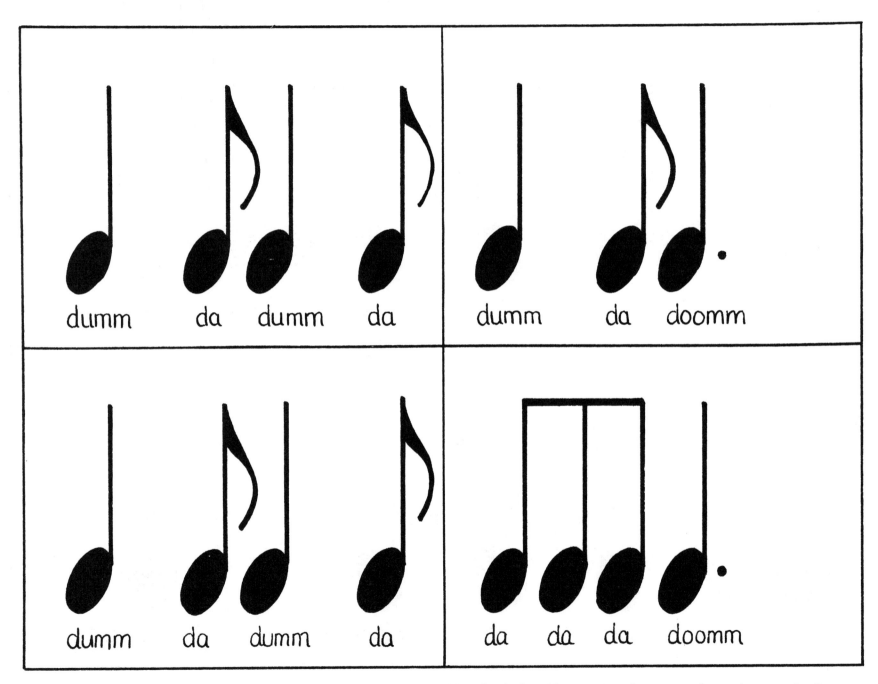

This page may be photocopied for use in the classroom and should not be declared in any return in respect of any photocopying licence.

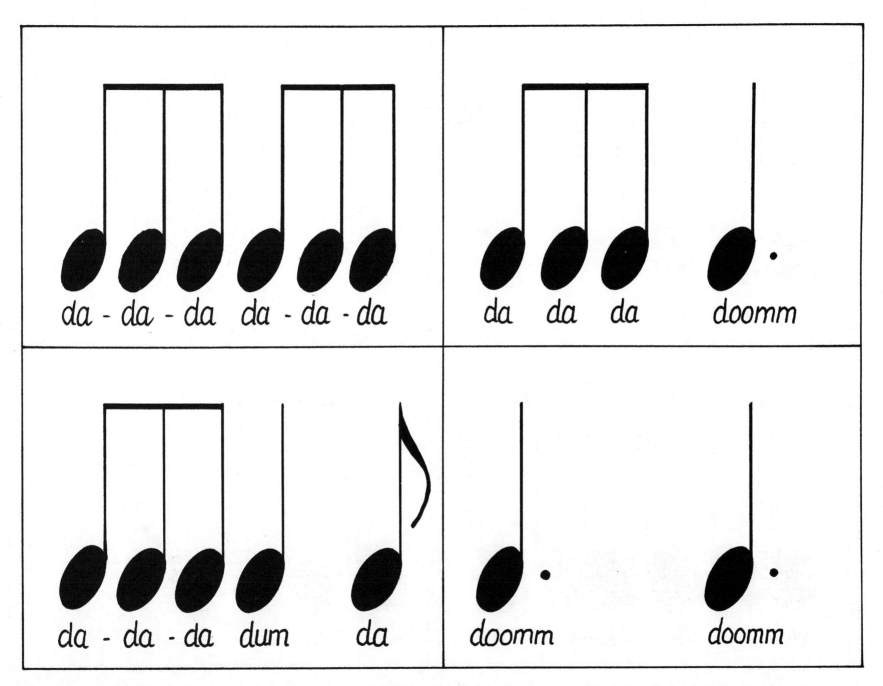

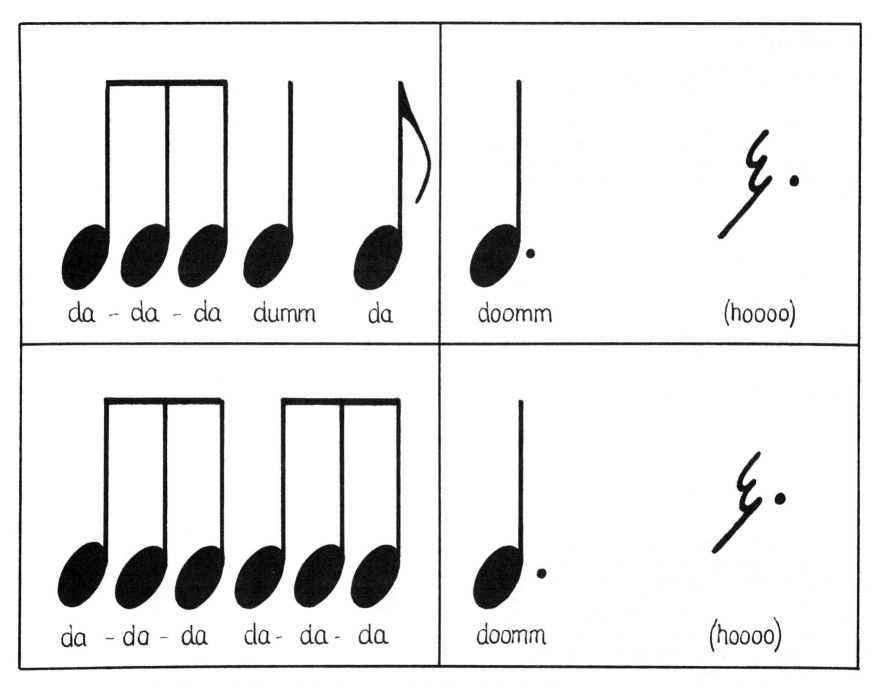

da – da – da   dumm   da   doomm   (hoooo)

da – da – da   da- da- da   doomm   (hoooo)

This page may be photocopied for use in the classroom and should not be declared in any return in respect of any photocopying licence.

Rhythms 2
4/4 (four four) time

The best way to acquire good rhythmic sense is by
listening and imitating. If you watch the appropriate signs
as you listen, you will almost certainly make the aural-
visual connection as well. Children do this without
explanation.

   The mathematical proportions are:

if ♩ represents one unit of time

   ♩ represents two units

   ♩. represents three units

   ♩ represents four units

So ♪ goes three times as fast as ♩.

   or twice as fast as ♩

   or four times as fast as ♩

   ♩ goes twice as fast as ♩

Only one type of rest (silence) is used. 𝄽 = ♩
   Children should watch and point at the cards as they
are chanted — never more than one card at a time to start
with.
   As they gain experience they can play from them,
improvise melodies from them, both vocally and
instrumentally; and when they use more than one,
arrange them in various orders.

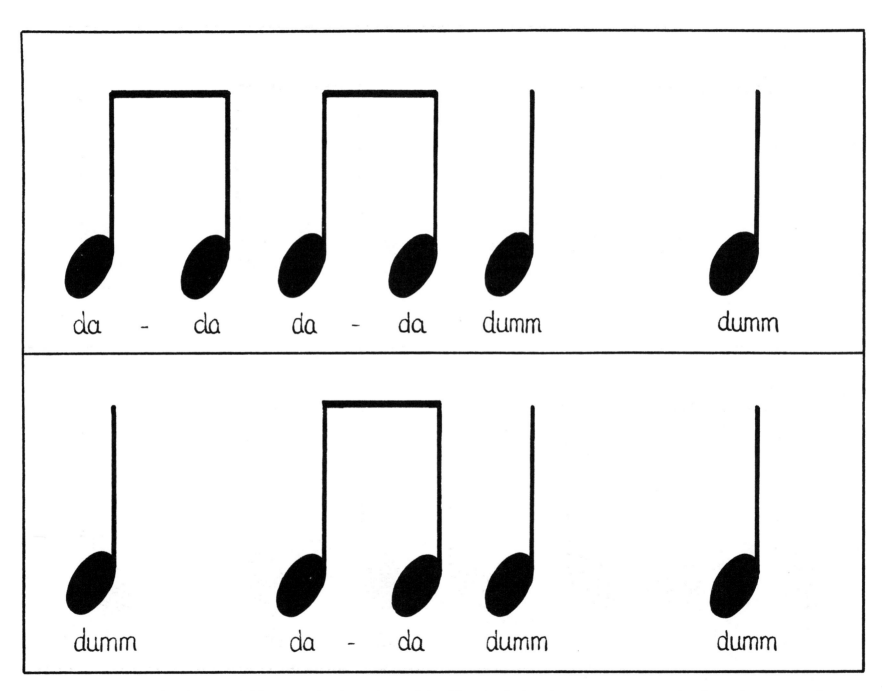

This page may be photocopied for use in the classroom and should not be declared in any return in respect of any photocopying licence.

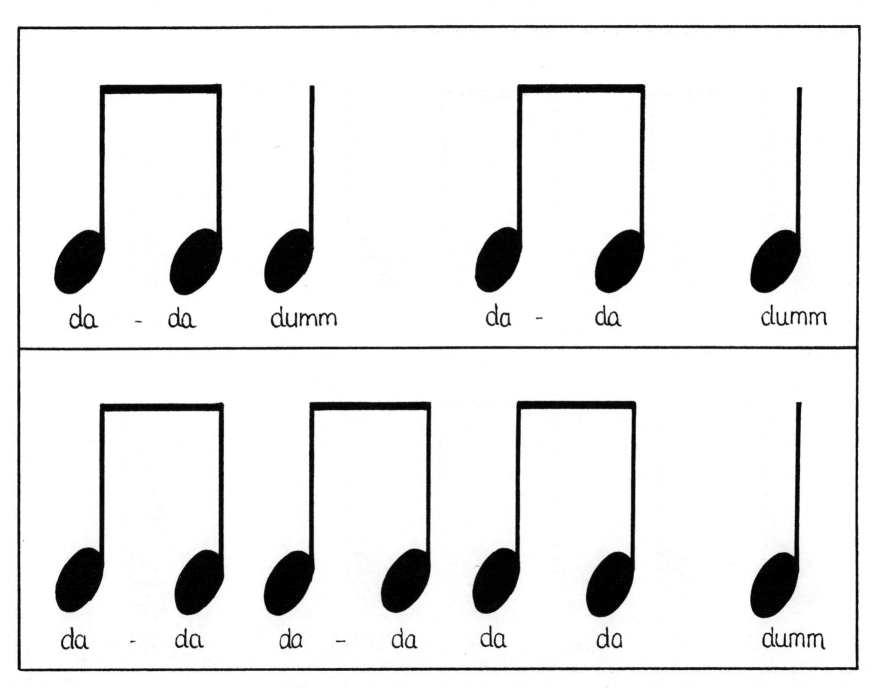

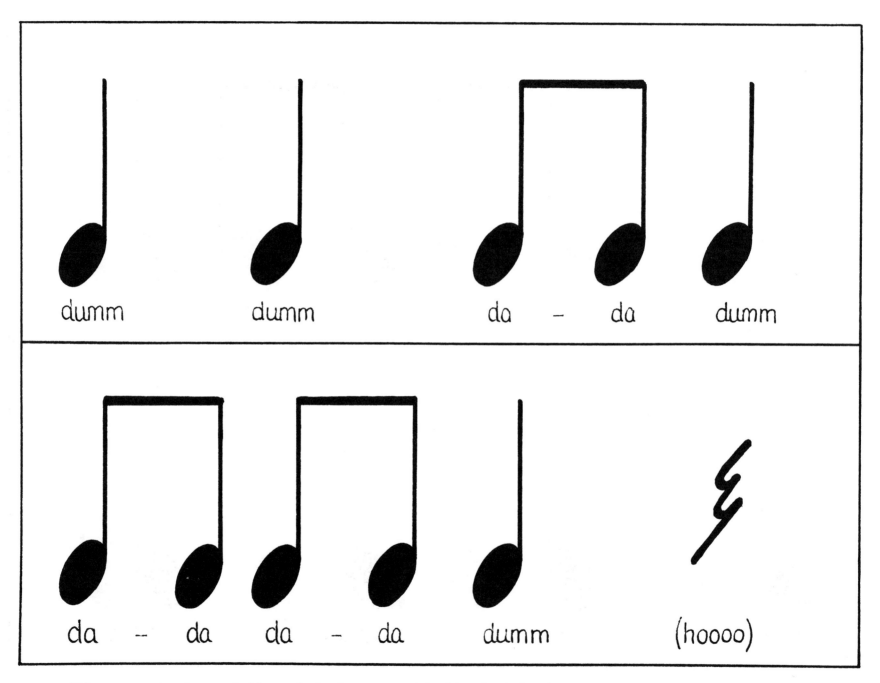

This page may be photocopied for use in the classroom and should not be declared in any return in respect of any photocopying licence.

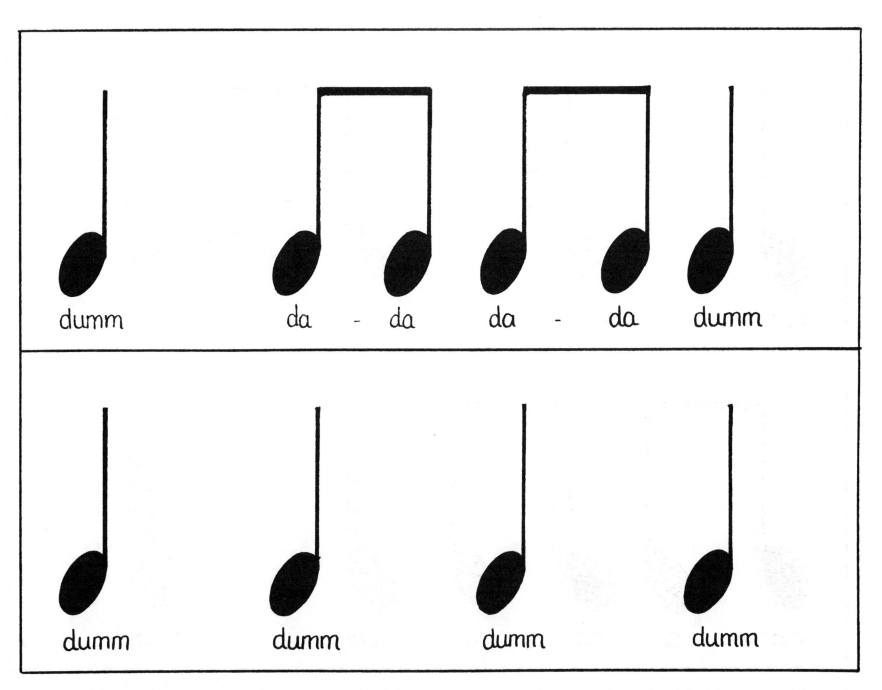

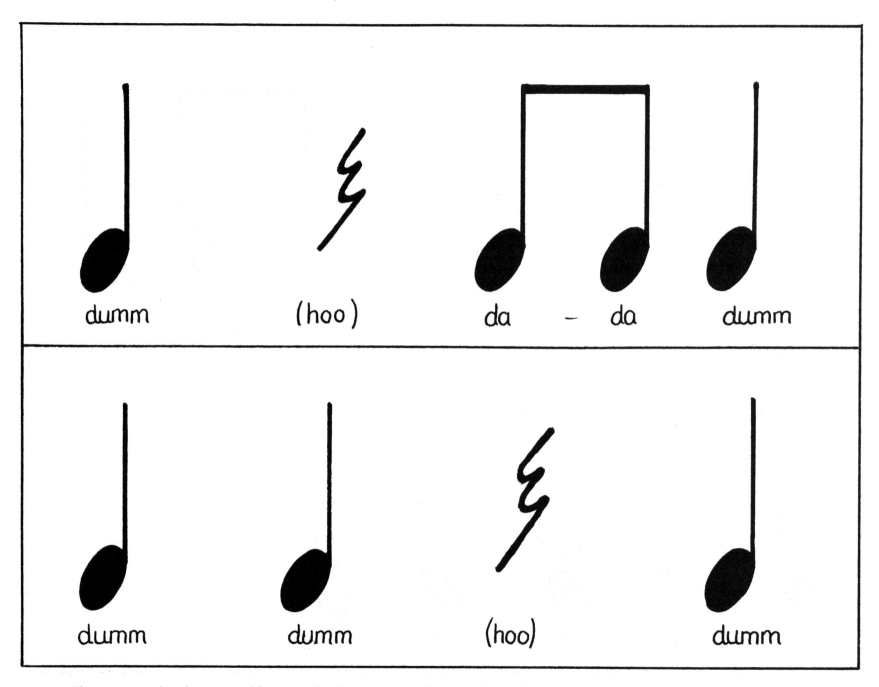

This page may be photocopied for use in the classroom and should not be declared in any return in respect of any photocopying licence.

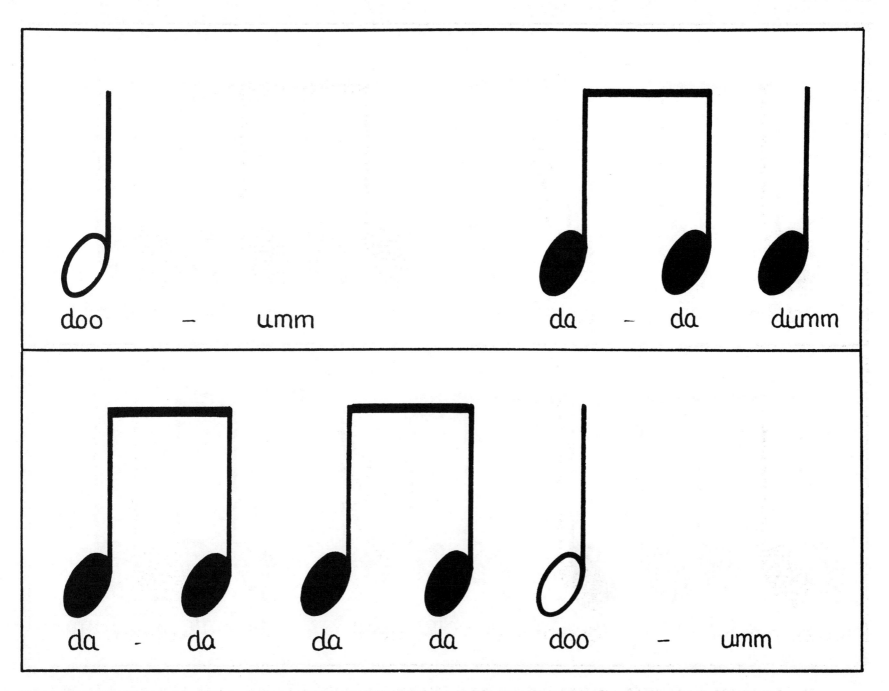

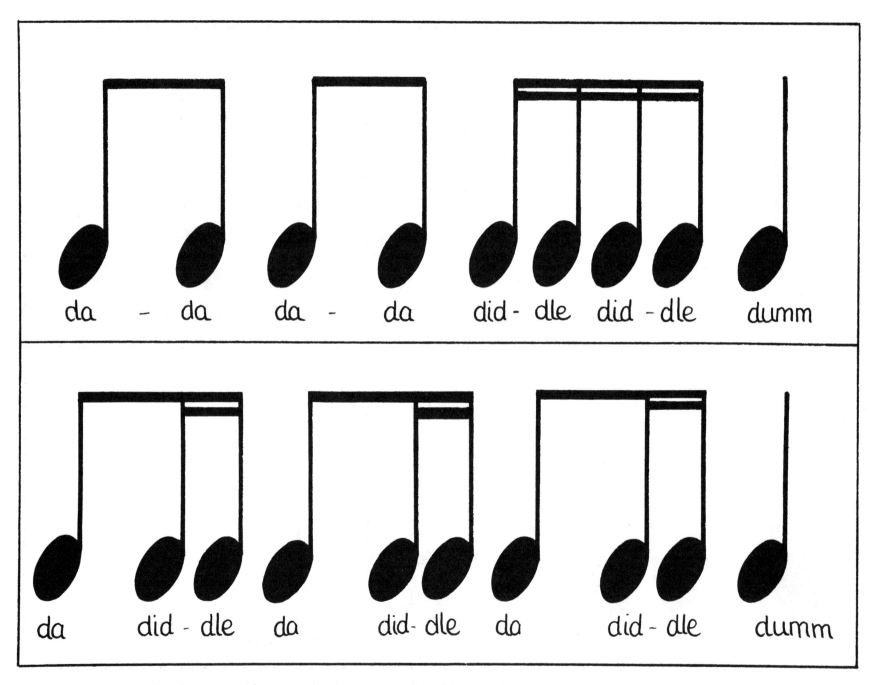

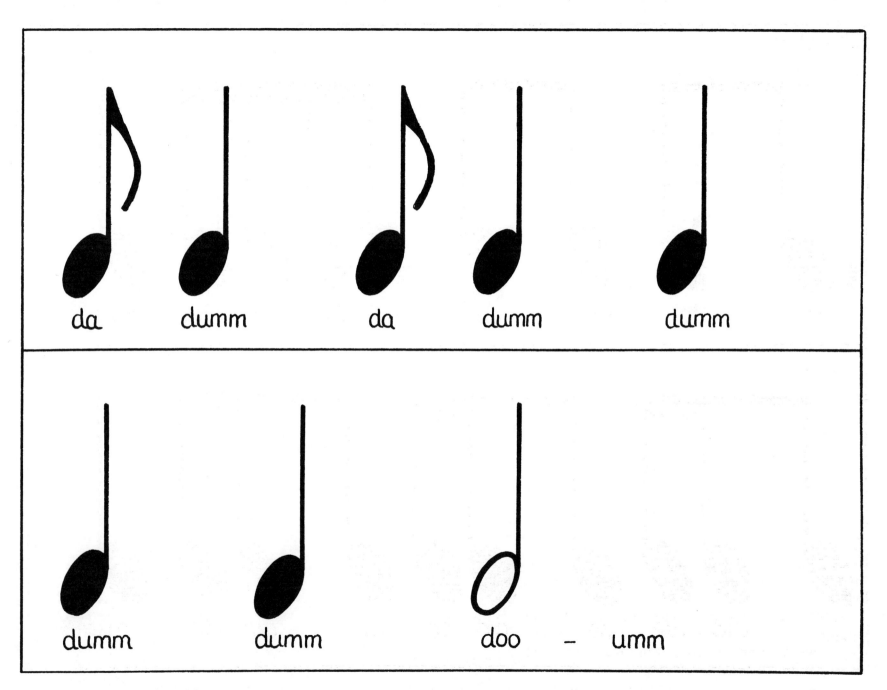

Rhythms 3
3/4 (three four) time

The best way to acquire good rhythmic sense is by listening and imitating. If you watch the appropriate signs as you listen, you will almost certainly make the aural-visual connection as well. Children do this without explanation.

The mathematical proportions are:

if ♪ represents one unit of time

♩ represents two units

♩. represents three units

♩ represents four units

So ♪ goes three times as fast as ♩.

or twice as fast as ♩

or four times as fast as ♩

♩ goes twice as fast as ♩

Only one type of rest (silence) is used. 𝄽 = ♩

Children should watch and point at the cards as they are chanted – never more than one card at a time to start with.

As they gain experience they can play from them, improvise melodies from them, both vocally and instrumentally; and when they use more than one, arrange them in various orders.

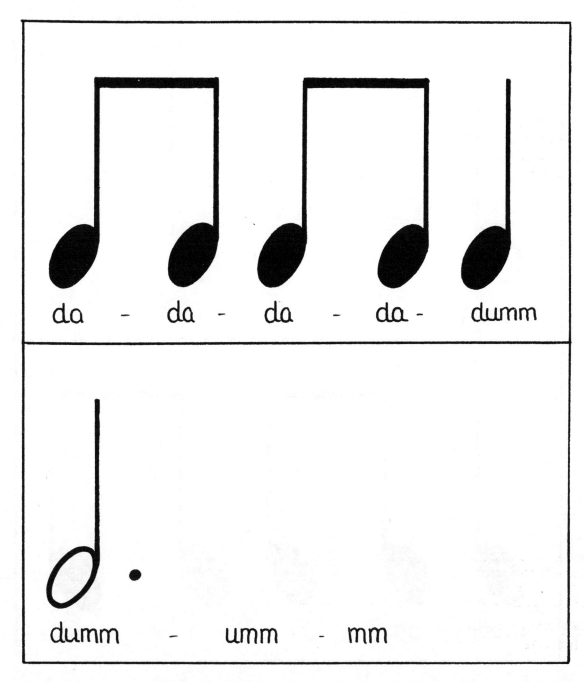

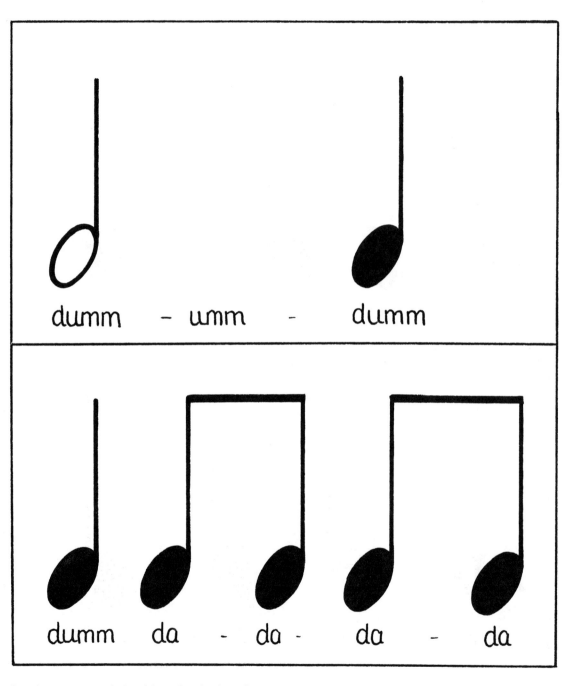

This page may be photocopied for use in the classroom and should not be declared in any return in respect of any photocopying licence.

Songs

These songs are written in 'Words on Staff' notation. This is intended to show children graphically how the words of a song change pitch. The words are accurately written where the blobs (●) would be in normal notation. Rhythms are written above. Even five-year-olds will be able to follow a song that they know.

Note: In normal notation words are written in a horizontal line under the music. Thus children tend to read the words and memorise the music. With this method they cannot help reading the music!

Pease pudding hot

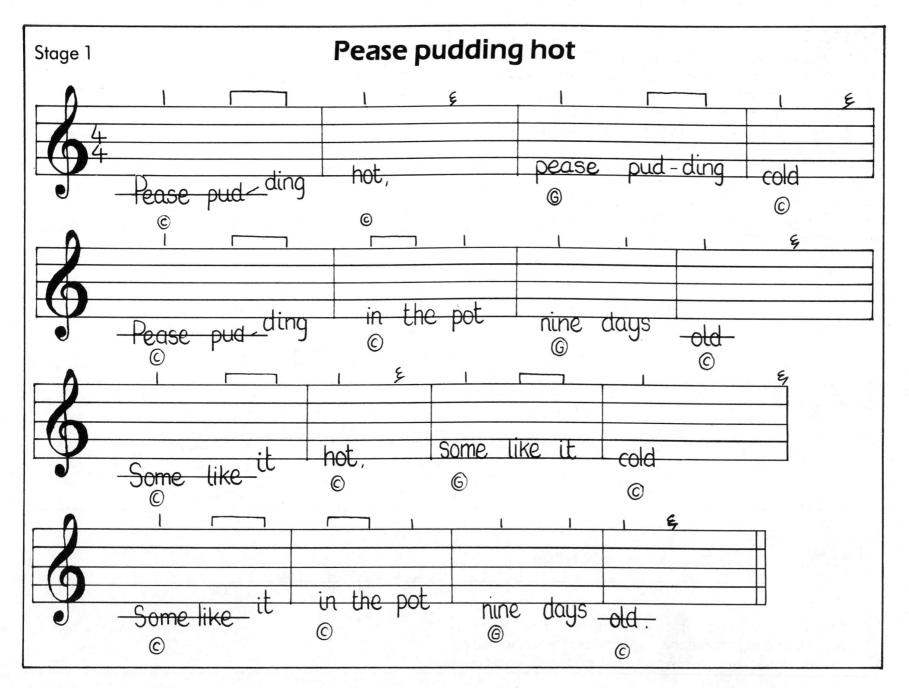

Stage 1

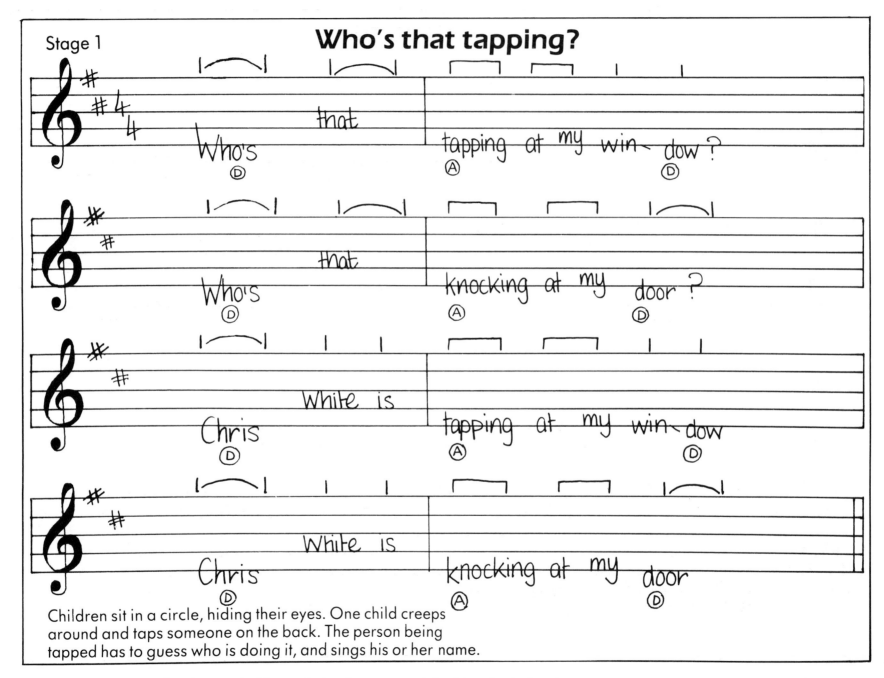

Who's that tapping at my win-dow?
Who's that knocking at my door?
Chris White is tapping at my win-dow
Chris White is knocking at my door

Children sit in a circle, hiding their eyes. One child creeps around and taps someone on the back. The person being tapped has to guess who is doing it, and sings his or her name.

Old woman

Stage 1

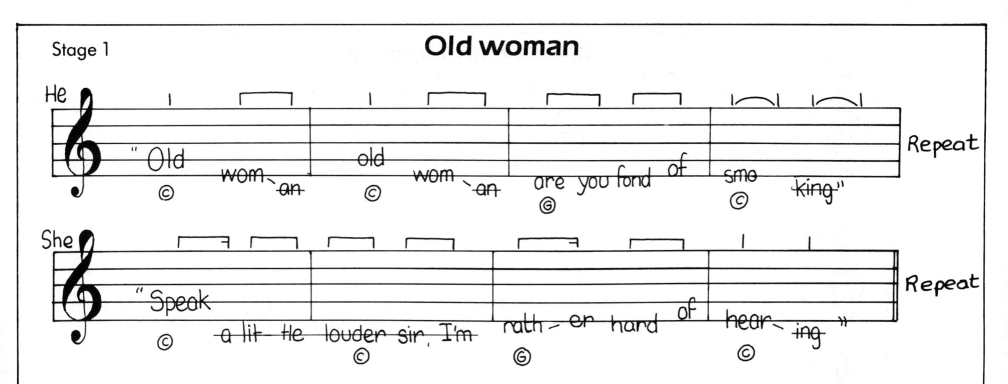

Verse 2
Old woman, old woman, are you fond of carding?
Speak a little louder sir, I'm rather hard of hearing.

Verse 3
Old woman, old woman, will you let me court you?
Speak a lit-tle louder sir, I just begin to hear you.

Verse 4
Old woman, old woman, will you let me marry you?
Thank you very kindly sir, I hear you very clearly.

Each line sing twice.

When I was a little boy

English folk song

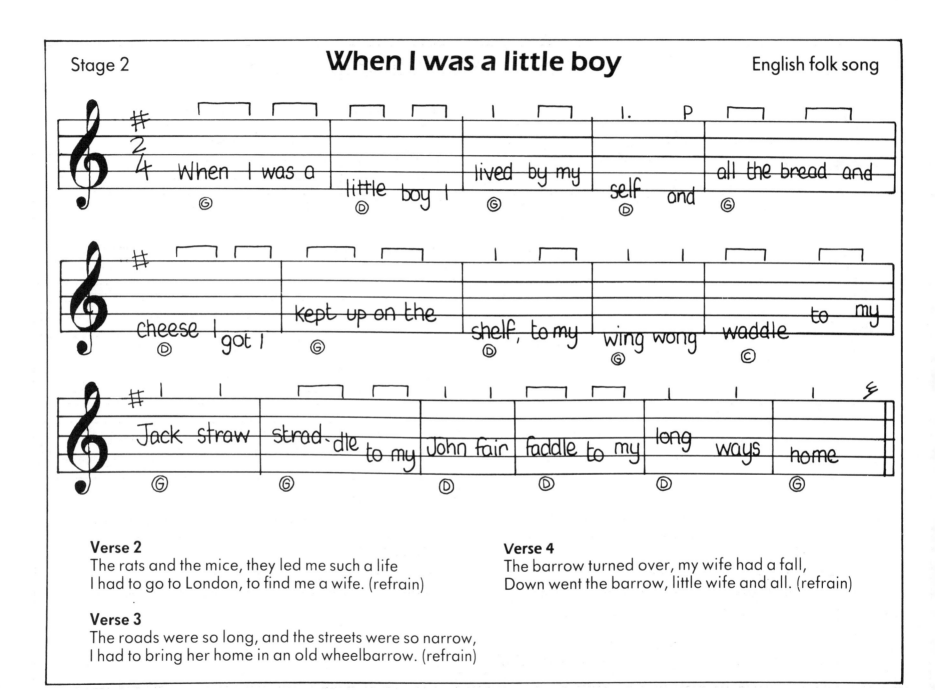

Verse 2
The rats and the mice, they led me such a life
I had to go to London, to find me a wife. (refrain)

Verse 3
The roads were so long, and the streets were so narrow,
I had to bring her home in an old wheelbarrow. (refrain)

Verse 4
The barrow turned over, my wife had a fall,
Down went the barrow, little wife and all. (refrain)

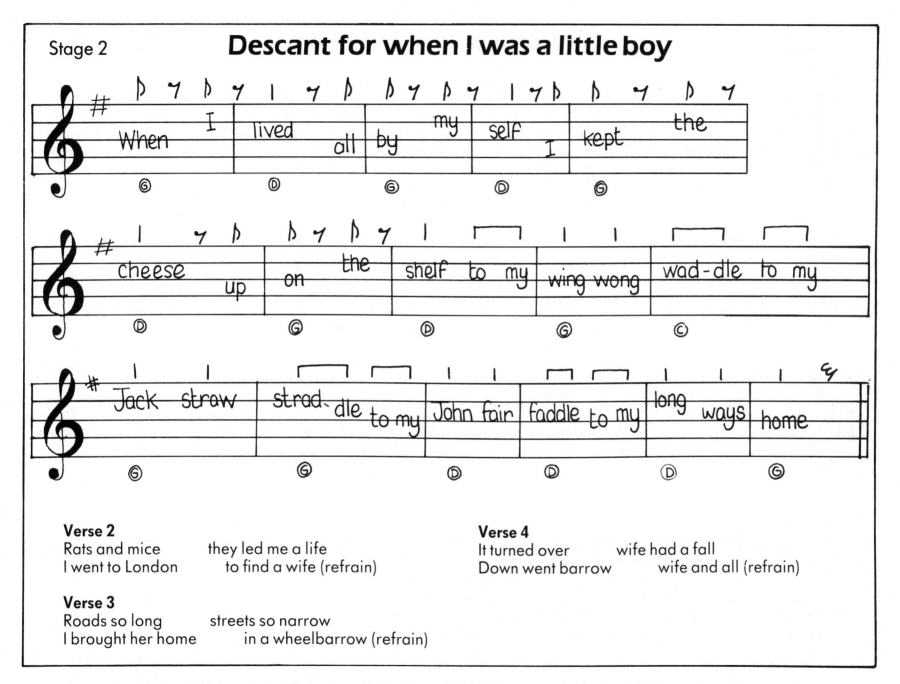

Stage 2

Descant for when I was a little boy

Verse 2
Rats and mice   they led me a life
I went to London   to find a wife (refrain)

Verse 3
Roads so long   streets so narrow
I brought her home   in a wheelbarrow (refrain)

Verse 4
It turned over   wife had a fall
Down went barrow   wife and all (refrain)

The tailor and the mouse

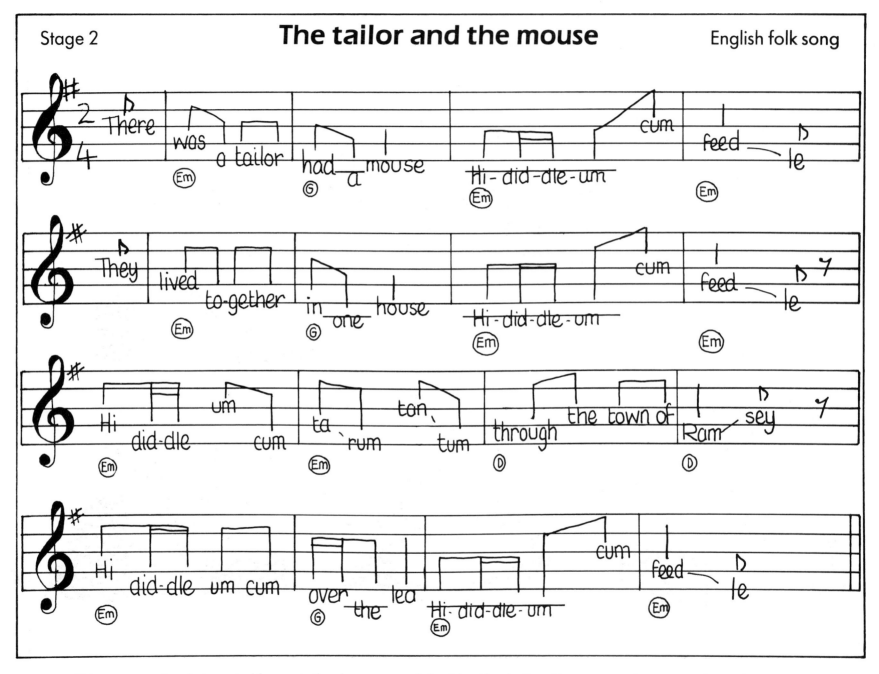

Verse 2
The tailor found his mouse was ill,
So he gave him part of a blue pill.

Verse 3
The tailor thought his mouse would die
So he baked him in a pie.

Verse 4
The pie was cut, the mouse ran out,
The tailor chased him all about.

Verse 5
The tailor found his mouse was dead,
So he bought another one instead.

Hee haw hum

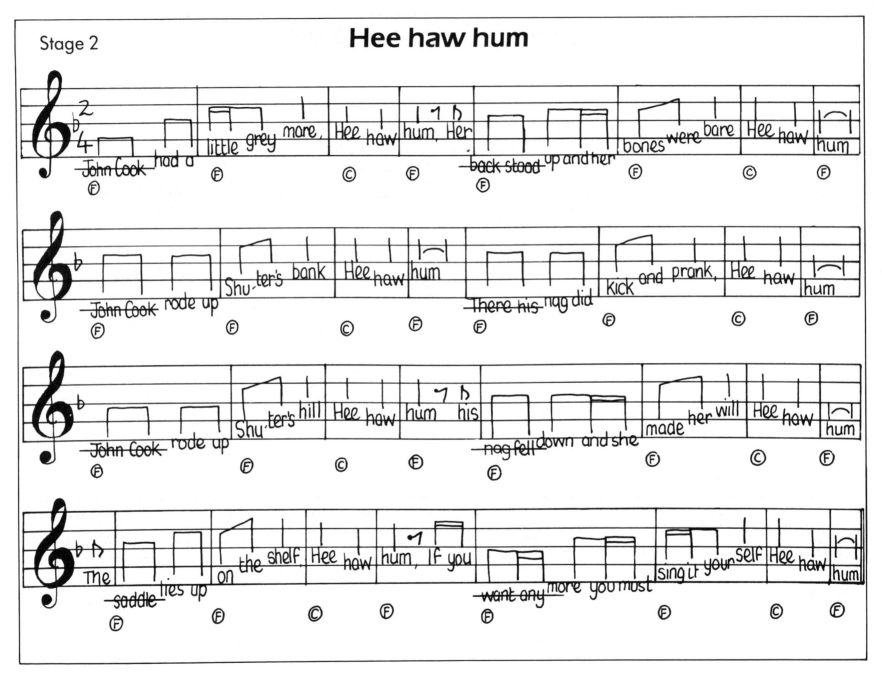

This page may be photocopied for use in the classroom and should not be declared in any return in respect of any photocopying licence.

Three small cars: a round

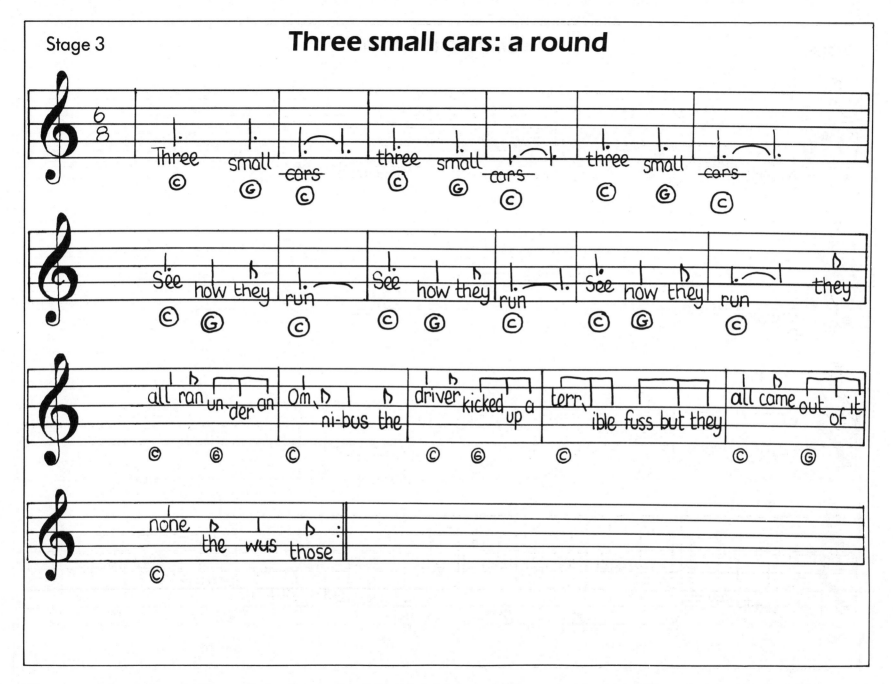

O sinner man

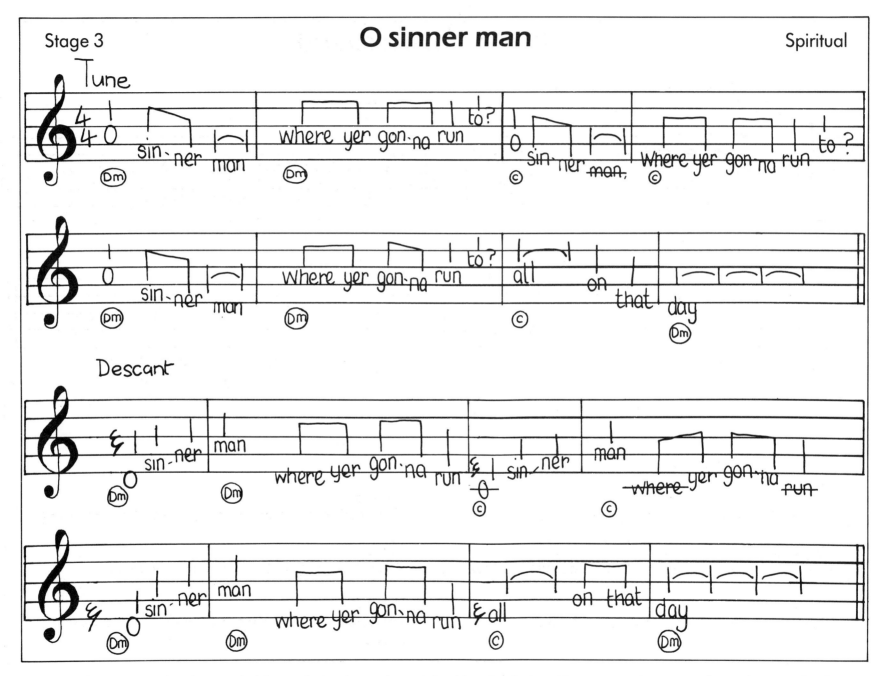

Kukaburra: a round

Round

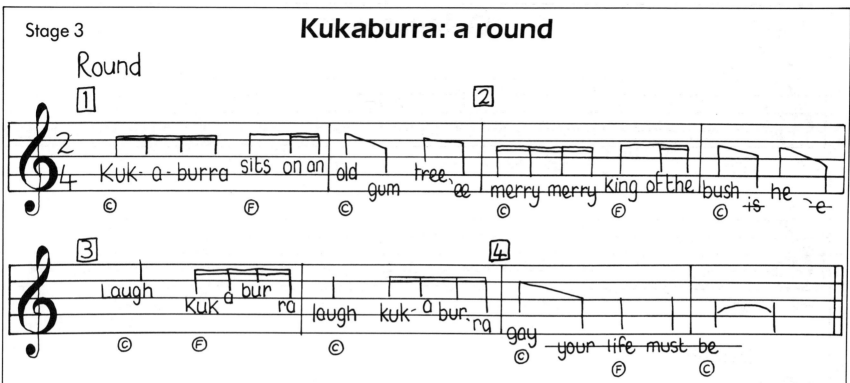

A Kukaburra is an Australian bird whose call is like laughter.

O sinner man

Verse 2
Run to the moon, 'O moon won't you hide me?'

Verse 3
The Lord said, 'O sinner man, the moon'll be a-bleeding.'

Verse 4
Run to the sea, 'O sea, won't you hide me?'

Verse 5
'The Lord said, 'O sinner man, the sea'll be a sin-king.'

Verse 6
Run to the Lord, 'O Lord, won't you hide me?'

Verse 7
The Lord said, 'O sinner man, wish you'd come home sooner.'

Colon man

Stage 3

West Indian folk song

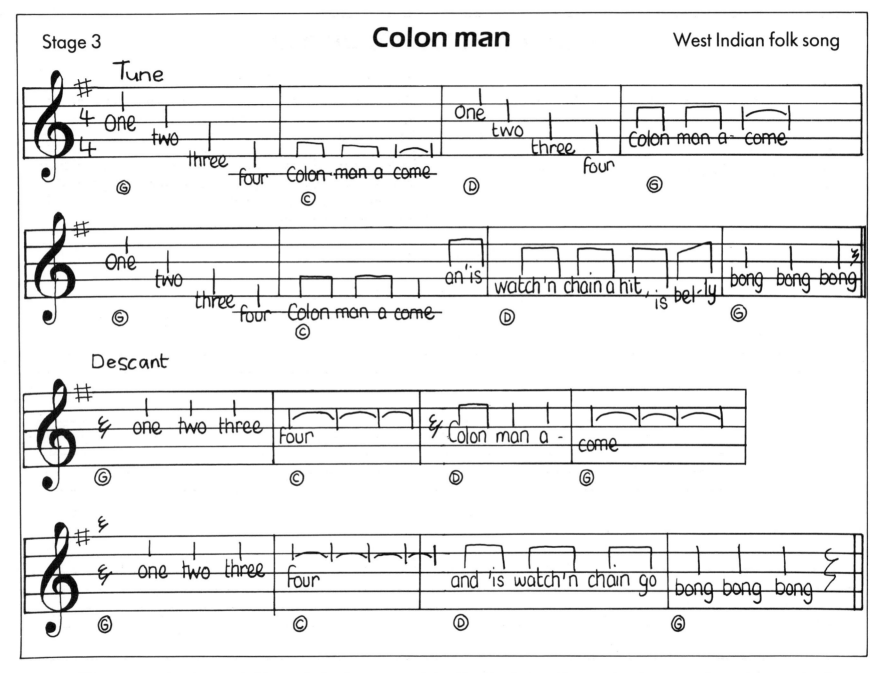

Second part for 'Colon man'

Verse 2
I ask him for a dollar and he give me back a dime.
(three times)

Verse 3
I asked him for the time and he look up at the sun.
(three times)

Verse 4
I think I'm going to Colon, going to make some money too.
(three times)

Note: West Indians in the early part of this century used to cross over to Colon to earn high wages, digging the Panama Canal. To show off their wealth, many would buy a watch and chain.

Music lined paper

Addison body notation

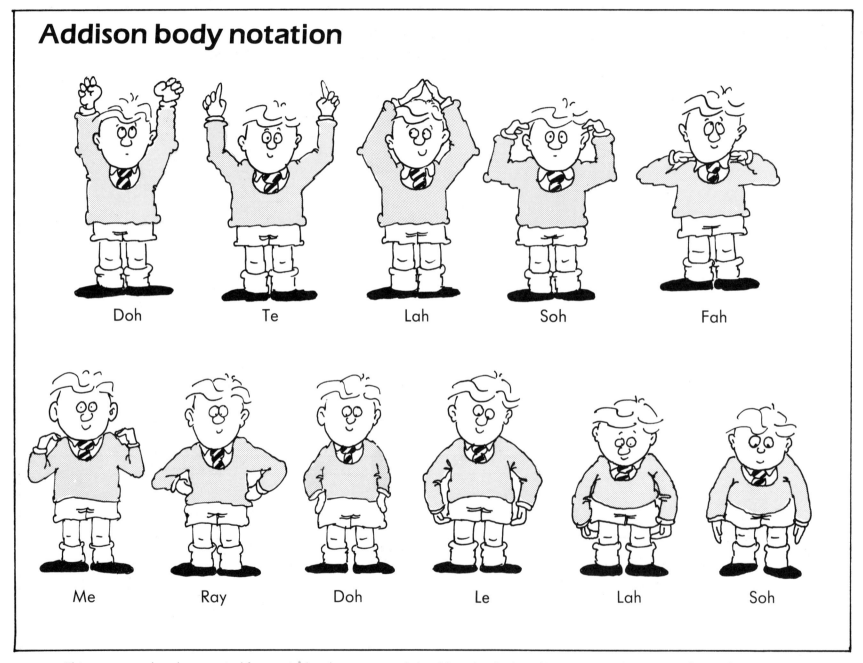

Doh   Te   Lah   Soh   Fah

Me   Ray   Doh   Le   Lah   Soh

Curwen hand signs

for further information see *The New Curwen Method*
W H Swinborne, Curwen Institute

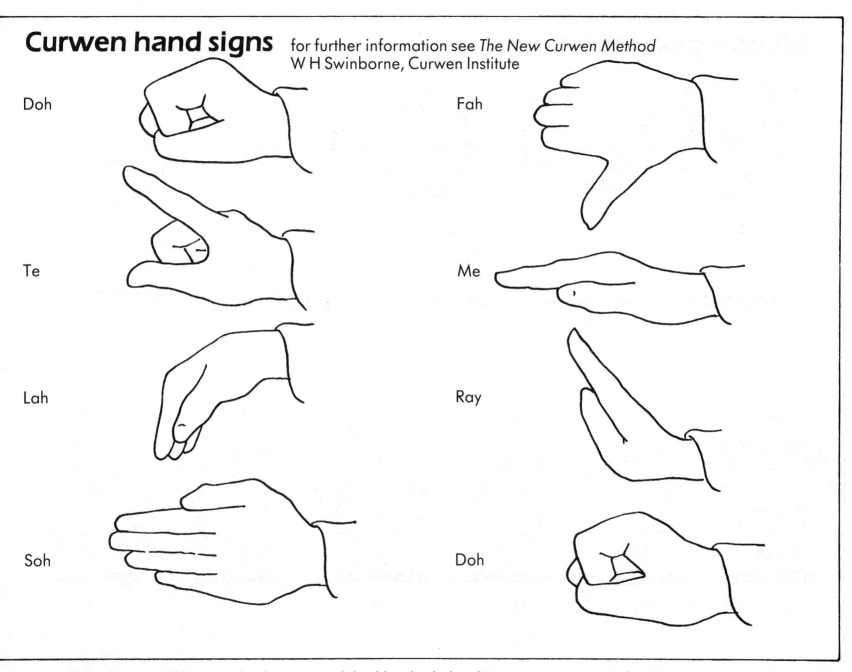

Doh

Te

Lah

Soh

Fah

Me

Ray

Doh

Acknowledgements

The publishers would like to thank the pupils of Sherburn Hill Infant School, Durham for the poems on page 45 and 46: 'The Waterfall', 'The Blacksmith', 'Autumn', 'The Coggle' and 'Winter'; and *Child Education* for Rhyme bank 2.

The publishers also gratefully acknowledge permission from the following sources to reproduce copyrighted material:
Cadbury Ltd for 'The River' by Susanna Taylor (6) Ecclesall Infant School, Sheffield from *Cadbury's Third Book of Children's Poetry* (Beaver Book), (see page 156).
A & C Black for 'The Giant' from *Acting Rhymes* Clive Sansom (see page 24).